Early Days Yet
New and Collected Poems 1941-1997

Early Days Yet

NEW AND COLLECTED POEMS 1941-1997

ALLEN CURNOW

CARCANET

First published in Great Britain in 1997 by
Carcanet Press Limited
4th Floor, Conavon Court
12-16 Blackfriars Street
Manchester M3 5BQ

A CIP catalogue record for this book
is available from the British Library
ISBN 1 85754 297 5

The publisher acknowledges financial assistance
from the Arts Council of England

Set in 10pt Palatino by Bryan Williamson, Frome.
Printed and bound in England by SRP Ltd, Exeter.

For Jeny

CONTENTS

The Game of Tag (1989-1997)

Continuum (1988)

The Loop in Lone Kauri Road (1986)

You Will Know When You Get There (1982)

An Incorrigible Music: a sequence (1979)

An Abominable Temper (1973)

Trees, Effigies, Moving Objects: a sequence (1972)

from *A Small Room with Large Windows* (1962)

from *Poems 1949 – 1957* (1957)

from *At Dead Low Water* (1949)

from *Sailing or Drowning* (1943)

from *Island and Time* (1941)

Notes / 241

ACKNOWLEDGEMENTS

Grateful acknowledgement is made to the journals in which some
of these poems first appeared: to *London Review of Books* for 'The
Unclosed Door', 'A South Island Night's Entertainment', 'Another
Week-end at the Beach', 'The Game of Tag', 'Looking West, Late
Afternoon, Low Water', 'The Scrap-book', 'Investigations at the
Public Baths', 'An Evening Light', and 'Pacific 1945-1995'; to
Partisan Review for 'The Vespiary: a Fable'; to *London Magazine* for
'Survivors', 'Continuum', 'Moules à la Marinière', 'Gare SNCF
Garavan', 'A Facing Page', 'The Ocean is a Jam Jar', and 'Early
Days Yet'; *Verse* for 'A Busy Port'; and *Sport* for the first New
Zealand appearance of several of these poems. Other poems first
appeared in *Encounter, P.N. Review,* the *Melbourne Age Monthly
Review,* the *Bulletin, Poetry* (Chicago), *Ariel, The Australian,* the *New
Zealand Listener, The Press, Islands, Landfall,* the *Times Literary
Supplement, Penguin New Writing.*

My special thanks are due to Auckland University Press, with
Oxford University Press, for letting me include here the poems
from collections published by them, in particular *Continuum, The
Loop in Lone Kauri Road, You Will Know When You Get There, An
Incorrigible Music,* and *A Small Room with Large Windows.*

This book is 'collected' in the sense of including everything I have
published since the 'sixties, along with my poems of the 'nineties,
collected here for the first time. From earlier decades, I have found
it a question less of selections than of omissions, leaving out what –
it seemed most likely – could as well be left behind for the present.

– A.C.

The Erewhonians say that we are drawn through life backwards; or again, that we go onwards into the future as into a dark corridor. Time walks beside us and flings back shutters as we advance; but the light thus given often dazzles us, and deepens the darkness which is in front. We can see but little at a time. . . . ever peering curiously through the glare of the present into the gloom of the future, we presage the leading lines of that which is before us, by faintly reflected lights from dull mirrors that are behind, and stumble on as we may till the trap-door opens beneath us and we are gone. . . . The Erewhonians say it was by chance only that the earth and the stars and all the heavenly worlds began to roll from east to west and not from west to east, and in like manner that man is drawn through life with his face to the past instead of to the future. For the future is there as much as the past, only that we may not see it. Is it not in the loins of the past, and must not the past alter before the future can do so?

Sometimes, again, they say that there was a race of men tried upon the earth once, who knew the future better than the past, but that they died in a twelvemonth from the misery which their knowledge caused them . . .

SAMUEL BUTLER, *Erewhon*

1

The Game of Tag
and Other Poems
(1989-1997)

THE UNCLOSED DOOR

Freshened by any wind, sanitised
with pine and cypress, the slaughterhouse

is cool as a church inside. High rafters
too. A gallery. The hooks hang ready.

Nothing else intercepts the day's late
blaze across the Seven Sleepers' chins

and Cooper's Knobs, on this point between
adjacent bays, only a blotched light

can get past, as the wind in the trees,
fidgeting to the doorway. The door

on its iron track having been wheeled back
wide enough, the small boys, me and Bob

Crawford, can see in. One of the men
turns our way, in the act of closing his

left hand on the lamb's throat, at the bass
viol the right, the bowing hand slashes

deep! *in blood stepped in so far* will up
to the eyes or the ears be enough?

They're all busy now, the hosing down
will have started. Add water and sweep

shit pellets puddled blood, the outfall
gulps, discharges over the rock-face

misting all the way to the green bay
water, with a noise of waters, where

the round stain dilates. An enrichment.
I think the children had been silent, all

this time. I will have pulled my bike, off
his, on the tree. Nothing alters this.

5   *The Game of Tag*

A SOUTH ISLAND NIGHT'S ENTERTAINMENT

Somebody mistook
the day, or how

will we have found
ourselves denied

entry, by chained
gate, padlocked

bolted door of an
empty dark shed

of a hall, miles
from the next town-

ship, as many from
the last lit lamp?

The night itself
unpunctuated,

no Southern Cross,
no Pointers, no

cartwheeling, hand-
standing giant

Orion, aka
Urine (born cauled

in a sacrificial
Boeotian cow's

pelt, pissed in by
no fewer than three

grateful gods) no
moon. Heavy cloud.

This my ninth year
under them all gets

darker by the minute.
What's visible here?

Not the crab tropic's
maidenliest stars

twinkle-twinkling
on my grandmother's

East Anglian
wedding night, swapped

now, for a sphere
beyond the circuit

of the shuddering Bear.
Eastward our austral

Pacific sands,
our high snows west-

ward. Our meridian
threads a chained gate

which brings us up
all standing, my father,

my mother, her
mother, and me.

Shut out. Wrong day.
Wrong side of the screen

where a New Age
was to have unreeled

itself, stormed this
barn in drizzling light.

Unreeled the fat
man's quaking back-

firing automobile.
Silent. His arse-

over-kite exit.
Silent. The Metro

Goldwyn lion's jaws
parted. A World

War One great gun
discharged. Silent.

A cloud that was
the city. A painted

scream. Silent, only
for the lady playing

'Rustle of Spring'
in an empty dark

shed of a hall.
Nobody comes.

Only our feet go
crunch-crunch in and out

of step as they fall,
all the way home.

A BUSY PORT

I

My turn to embark. A steep gangplank
expects me. An obedient child,
I follow my father down.

It happens that the sun will have topped
a black hill beside the time-ball tower,
and found the spot of a fresh

tear on Bob Hempstalk's cheekbone, whose wet
red eyes blink back seaward where he leans
for'ard at the wheel-house glass;

one hand wipes an eye, the other shakes
a half-hitch loose, unlashing the wheel.
A man's tears, obscene to me

caught looking. Too late now. The time-ball
drops. Quayside voices (not for my ears)
discuss the dead, bells repeat

ding-ding across the wharf. Brightwork traps
the sun in brass when I next look up,
following my father down,

who made the trip himself many years
past. The old rust-bucket gets up steam.
Frequent sailings from where we live.

II

Winched aboard still warm over the for'ard
hatch the morning's bread hangs by a breath
of its own. It smells of bed.

An enriched air. The urinal under
the wharf drip-feeds, the main steam below
sweats. Darky Adams, deckhand

engineer stoker bangs his firebox
open, slings in a shovelful, slams
the insulted flame back home,

thick acrid riddance topples the way
smoke rolls by its own weight, in an air
that barely lifts, off the stack.

One jump clear of the deck the plank dips
with a short uneasy motion, deep-
sea talk to the paddler's foot

out of my depth, deeper yet, off the Heads,
our Pillars. Pitching like a beer-can.
I'm hanging on tight, can't hear

clashes from the stokehole for the wind
yelling, crossed on the wheel he's yelling
back, 'Ay, bit of a stiff breeze'.

Eyes that last I saw in tears can read
abstruse characters of waves, on course
between them, our plunging bows.

ANOTHER WEEKEND AT THE BEACH

Turn left at the sign. Lone Kauri Road
winds down to the coast. That's a drop
of about five hundred feet. Look out
for the waterfall, the wooden bridge,
the mown grass, the pohutukawa glade.

The western horizon will have slid
behind the mask of an eye-levelled
next eyeballing wave. Park here. Proceed
on foot. The spot has barbecues with
MALE and FEMALE dunnies in a figtree

thicket, wrong hemisphere, implausibly
fruiting. Tracks cross the wind-sifting dune
skyline of unkempt lupin, marram,
spinifex's incontinent seed-
vessels bowling downwind, the way I've

come and come, how many thousand times
to no other conclusion, the back
of a broken wave, and found no word
or forgot or omitted to write
it down, *Ah, quelle écriture de la*

différance! l'orthographe derridienne
for every thing's everything. Then why
not phytoplankton, the algoid bloom
any less than those offshore purples, this
beached medusa, polythene waste, bubbled

sea-froth, tincture of a present spume
spattered up the sands? Mind where you pick
your mussels and *kina*, these tides may
secrete indigenous toxins. Deadly
to the text. Shall I copy it again?

THE GAME OF TAG

AFRIKA POET HERO DODGER FELIX DEVOE CURSE EXIT
CICERO BEASTIE SAINT THANKS FOR THE TAG AFRIKA POET '93
Graffito, Lone Kauri Road

Seven thigh-thick
hamstring-high posts,

embedded two
metres and cemented

in, where the side
of the road burst

into bird space,
tree-toppling all

that plunging way
down. A clean-cut

horizon shapes
daylight. A gap.

Where the sea glares
back at the land's

shiftiness. Hefty
planks mounted strap-

wise, post to post,
invite my spray-

gun-toting rival
to sign A-F-R-I-K-A

P-O-E-T-92
who will have caught

up with himself
at the next bend

where the road slipped
again, and again

tagged the white paint-
edness of a new

barrier A-F-R-I-K-A
P-O-E-T-93. The paint

is for the poetry.
And signed off. Skid

marks in the gravel.
And powered the old

Falcon around, like
a bat out of Hell. Gave

Death the fingers.
Shook the dreadlocks

from his eyes, for
his best shot. Darkly

incontinently
lets fly, spattering

name after name.
A crumbling road.

Where have they all
gone, with CICERO

BEASTIE and me
and which of us

leads the way down
post and plank not-

withstanding, car-
apaced in Korean

steel, to be wrapped
round a bole two

hundred years thick,
two hundred feet

below. One wild
wheelie and we're off.

Rain-forest soon
repairs its ruins.

Dead men's dental
records and cellphones

tell no lies. Rust
finishes the job

(almost). One chip
of red Perspex

under a stone
in the stream was

his (whose?) tail-light.
A-F-R-I-K-A P-O-E-T

writes, and I quote
THANKS FOR THE TAG.

LOOKING WEST, LATE AFTERNOON, LOW WATER

*The typical tidal range, or difference in sea level between high and low
tides, in the open ocean is about 2 ft (0.6m), but it is much greater near
the coasts.*

Desk encyclopedia

Our beach was never so bare. Freak tide,
system fault, inhuman error, will it

never stop falling? After dark, said
the tables of high water and sunset

pasted on the wall, which don't deceive.
Come on down for a walk while there's light.

A wall of pale green glass miles above
head high alongside, complete with fish

crossing, is what will have been the wave
once it has broken. Leviathan is

the beached cachalot we left Bob Falla
filleting for science, the ebb to wash

away these fifty years, each one smaller
than the last. Come down, this is today

delivered factory fresh, in colour
heated by the late sun. Time to try

looking on the bright side, or join those
Great God! (says the poem) who'd *rather be*

suckled in a creed outworn: but whose
cast-off cult's to be the lucky one?

Great waters, unfinished business, done
blind to the deadline. From that rock to

this tree was *tapu* and it sticks. Thin
pickings, Tangaroa, this is *pakeha*

story time, only Okeanos and
sister Tethys having it off: the way

they love makes hairy cliff-hanging seas
roll drums on the sand, the three-metre swell

flat on the seabed bangs the pubes,
very ancient and fishlike they smell

close to. Divine all the same. Dangerous,
not to be approached, least of all by

mortal man whose years are four-score plus
tomorrow night. While I count the three

strong swimmers carried past out of sight
round the North Rocks the whole shoreline shakes

underfoot again, dead friends call out
not to be heard. Look west, what looks

back is blood-orange nightfall, the stooped
sky drowning another sun overboard

15   *The Game of Tag*

where the horizon was: till it snapped
those deep-sea moorings and will be heard

oncoming, the sound of a scream. *tsunami!*
tsunami! splintering deadwood of the boat

I lost half a life ago, swept
away with a judgment on the work

she's amateur built but your friends won't know.
Last seen, one inflatable rescue

craft stood on its tuck, bows to skyward
in fast failing light, a turning tide.

THE SCRAP-BOOK

I

The light in the window blew out in a strong
draught only to return wearing a black mask,
behind William Woon's chair, which he draws up close

to the desk. A roundhouse swing from the nor'east
rocks the plank walls from blocks to purlins. He trims
the Miller Vestal's ragged flame, lays the scrap-

book open by the burning oil, finds a clean
pen, writes *Detained* (flourishing the big D)
at the Mata, Mr Monro's, during a gale

of wind, October 4, 1841.
Blood sample of Peter Monro, where do I
come in? The book doesn't say. Might as well ask

this heart-murmur I've got, how Edinburgh rock,
chipped like a golf ball cleared Arthur's Seat the day
after Waterloo, first bounce Van Diemen's Land,

holed up next and last a thousand sea miles more,
Ngapuhi country, MacGulliver's last landfall.
Not by this light. The rain pisses down, the tide

crawls up the creek, reads the mangroves' million false
scents. No way out of the Mata but by water
neither gig nor canoe can live in tonight.

II

Puts pen to the recto, lovers have left no room
on the verso, who damply dream of gravestones
and each other's names *May mine alone attract*

thy pensive eye! On a night like this, God help
poor sailors and lovers too, and the Reverend
William, who wishes it all further. As if

the Mata weren't further than ever God's writ
ran till the day before yesterday, and He
outnumbered thousands to one by the *iwi*

of the *tangata whenua*, and outgunned since
the musket spoke with tongues, not without a bang.
And writes against the wind, fishing for a poem

gilled in the drift-net of his mind, and pulls up
'Music', hymnodist Wesley's ghostly sixain
warning! Addiction can endanger the soul

and steal our hearts away from Thee. And subjoins
The Saviour, lover of storm-bound souls, starred
twice with a criss-cross ink-blot, *In Hoc Signo.*

III

Lifts the pen and listens for the wrath to come.
Hears nothing but the clock striking some small hour,
the crack of a *kauri* branch dropped by the gale.

17   *The Game of Tag*

The lovers are as dead as they ever dreamed.
Mildew has freckled the page, dulled the once-gilt
edge, browned the black longhand. All the lights are out,

it's blowing like the hammers, the power lines are down.
The scrap-book sheds loose pictures of lost homelands,
times long past, northern steeples and thatch, Maori

stockades. *Detained at the Mata*, what else does
the book say? The radio confides the latest
rape and Rugby. Another branch thumps the roof.

EARLY DAYS YET

1
Lift out front seat-
cushion. Unscrew
filler-cap. Insert

large funnel. Spike,
and up-end four gallon
can of Big Tree

Motor Spirit. Let
flammable contents
flow *pingle-pangle-*

pingle through fine
gauze filter. Your new
1919

Model T is now
fuelled for the week's
pastoral mileage,

Hororata, Kowai
Bush, Darfield. Three
Holy Communions per

gallon today (Sunday)
and by the time we
bury old Mrs. Hole

(Tuesday, Halswell
Churchyard) not much
left in the tank. Still,

miles better than the doctor's
barge-size guzzler,
and the right image

for the poor *The Lord be
with you* the pews creak back
And with thy spirit.

2

This world's the one
you are in. Replace
front seat-cushion.

Advance Throttle (on
left of steering-column)
and Spark (on right)

a few notches. Walk
to front, pull Choke
wire, engage starting-

handle, swing vigorously
up, release the moment
motor fires, and fires.

*A great while ago
the world began, with
hey, ho* Bang!

And where will it all
have ended? That
was a great way off.

3

This corrugated
iron outbuilding
doubles for cowbail,

garage. In a manger
Cow Beauty tongues
her rock-salt, rolls

the big lump over, and
over the milk-pail
my mother's hands

tug, squeeze, tug *pingle*
pangle. The New Age
enters, in reverse

gear, my father at the
wheel brakes, gets back
in gear, turns towards

Torlesse Range which is
twice blue, once for the
noon sky, deeper again

for the *massif*. No time
at all, that straight
lonely road locks us

both in with a high
head wind, unhingeing
nor'west slammer. I don't

see him any more
distinctly, for
dust of the earth,

his own. It closes
behind. The spirit
fires. Driving, driven,

swaying, keeps time with
his body, old habit.
Any old song the

motor beats out finds
words in his head
O forest, green

and fair, O pine-
tree, waving high,
How sweet your cool

retreat, How fresh
and fair A great
way off's too near

by far, the dust's
at our eyes already,
with a high warm wind,

with a whiff of japanned
seat-cushion, a shudder
with a skitter of rubber

on a rutted macadam,
with hey, ho, Bang!
And with thy spirit.

A FACING PAGE

Behind the eyelids the giant in the sky
is probably sightless, but that can't be known.

Cruciform from full-stretched arms his black robe drops
the whole way to the city. His fingers point

down at our rooftops. We don't know about him.
He knows all about us. By the fire the child's

nightgown is warmed for bed. The book's entitled
Under the Sunset by Bram Stoker M.A.

my mother's copy in green cloth board 8vo
has nearly lost the spine, a few threads hold,

her childhood and mine. Tucked and kissed for the dark,
I shut my eyes too tight on a picture-book

for waking to loosen. Locked on to where people
believe in themselves, engraved fingers point down.

INVESTIGATIONS AT THE PUBLIC BATHS

At nine fifteen a.m.
on the first day of his eighty-
first year. Why don't I

first-person myself?
I was hoping nobody would ask
me that question

yet. The strong smell of
chlorine for one thing, one thing
at a time, please.

For instance, there's always
this file of exercyclists
riding the gallery

over the pool. Bums
on saddles, pommelled crotches.
The feet rotate, the

hands grip, or hang
free, or hold open a book,
demonstrating how

the mind is improved
without progression, if not without
rumbling noises and

lascivious absences.
How free-standing engines enjoy
their moving parts,

privately mounted
overhead. There's also the deep
and the shallow end

between which the body
swims and the mind, totally
immersed, counts

and keeps count. I think
sixteen, touch tiles, turn again,
with underwater eyes

follow the black line.
Touch, thinking seventeen, turn
thinking eighteen

and enough. Whatever's
thinkable next or only the peg
where I last hang

my clothes. A destination.
The gallery rumble-trembles, the riders
always up there were

an abstraction blooded, a
frieze the wrong side of the urn.
One grins, catching

me looking, lifts
a tattooed hand. I wave back. So.
You know how it is.

PACIFIC 1945–1995

A Pantoum

. . . if th'assassination
could trammel up the consequence, and catch,
with his surcease, success; that but this blow
might be the be-all and the end-all . . . . here,
but here, upon this bank and shoal of time
we'ld jump the life to come . . .

– Macbeth

Quantifiable griefs. The daily kill.
   One bullet, with his name on, his surcease.
'The casualties were few, the damage nil' –
The scale was blown up, early in the piece.

One bullet, with his name on, his surcease.
   Laconic fire, short work the long war mocks.
The scale was blown up, early in the piece –
How many is few? After the aftershocks,

laconic fire – short work! The long war mocks,
   dragging out our dead. What calibration says
how many is few, after the aftershocks
of just such magnitude? We heard the news,

dragging out our dead. What calibration says,
   right! You can stop crying now, was it really
of just such magnitude? We heard the news
again, the statistical obscene, the cheery

right! You can stop crying now, was it really
   the sky that fell, that boiling blue lagoon?
Again, the statistical obscene, the cheery
salutation and bright signature tune.

The sky that fell! That boiling blue lagoon!
   Jacques Chirac's rutting tribe – with gallic
salutation and bright signature tune –
thermonuclear hard-on. Ithyphallic

Jacques! Chirac's rutting tribe, with gallic
    eye for the penetrable, palm-fringed hole –
thermonuclear hard-on, ithyphallic
    BANG! full kiloton five below the atoll.

Eye for the penetrable, palm-fringed hole,
    whose trigger-finger, where he sat or knelt down –
BANG! full kiloton five, below the atoll
    had it off, bedrock deep orgasmic meltdown –

whose trigger-finger, where he sat or knelt down,
    fifty years back, fired one as huge as then
had it off bedrock deep, orgasmic meltdown –
    whose but Ferebee's? – Hiroshima come again! –

fifty years back, fired one as huge as then
    fireballed whole cities while 'People . . . copulate, pray . . .'
Whose but Ferebee's – Hiroshima come again! –
    bombardier, U.S. Army? *Enola Gay*

fireballed whole cities while 'People . . . copulate, pray . . .'
    Not God fingering Gomorrah but the man,
bombardier, U.S. Army. *Enola Gay*
    shuddering at 30,000 feet began –

not God fingering Gomorrah, but the man,
    the colonel her pilot who named her for his Mom –
shuddering at 30,000 feet began –
    'Little Boy' delivered – her run for home:

the colonel her pilot, who named her for his Mom,
    flew her to roost (at last) in the Smithsonian.
'Little Boy' delivered, her run for home
    lighter by the Beast's birth, her son's companion:

flew her to roost (at last) in the Smithsonian:
    are tourists' hearts and hopes, viewing her there,
lighter by the Beast's birth, her son's companion?
    Jacques' Marianne's delivery, is that near?

Are tourists' hearts and hopes, viewing her there,
    pronounced infection-free and safely tested –
Jacques' Marianne's delivery, is that near? –
    What effluent, what fall-out's to be trusted?

pronounced infection-free and safely tested
    for carcinogenic isotope unseen fall-out –
what effluent, what fall-out's to be trusted?
    The Beast once born, who's answering the call-out?

For carcinogenic isotope, unseen fall-out,
    for the screaming city under the crossed hairs,
the Beast once born. Who's answering the call-out?
    no time even to know it's one of THEIRS –

for the screaming city under the crossed hairs,
    'The casualties were few, the damage nil' – ?
No time even to know! It's one of theirs –
    quantifiable griefs. The daily kill.

October – November 1995

AN EVENING LIGHT

The sun on its way down torched the clouds and left
them to burn themselves out on the ground:

the north-west wind and the sun both drop at once
behind the mountains. The foreground fills

with a fallen light which lies about the true
colours of absconded things, among

which I place this child whose tenth birthday happens
to have been my father's, that will be

a hundred years next Thursday. We were to meet
at a time of precisely such radiant

discolorations, the city of his mind.
The smallest leaf's alight where he looks

at the riverside willows, the painted iron
glows cold where he holds the garden gate.

The butcher's horse drops golden turds which steam
in sundown chill, an old man minds where

he walks, whose viridescent black assigns him
to an age before the city was,

I take his (my father's) hand: we follow him,
bowler hat, silver-topped stick, the hand

knuckled into the small of his back, which aches
to think of riding wet to the girths

and stirrups cutting up a country the size
of England with a sackful of pegs.

Under the one fallen firelit sky the Ngai-tahu
kainga and excavated *paa*

mark time by moa-bone middens, oceanic
migrations. What gospel will my father

preach to Tuahiwi, counting communicants
and the collection? A lamp-post cab-horse

blows into its nosebag, the old man fumbles
at his fob, his gold Waterbury's right

by the Post Office clock. By this light the city
is instant history, my father's mind.

Continuum
(1988)

SURVIVORS

Night falls on an unusual scene of public
rejoicing. A whole head taller than the crowd,

astride my father's nape, I can see the *jets
d'eau* the fire brigade pumps across the lake,

ebulliently spouted, illuminated.
Rose-coloured spectaculars blown to waterdrops

float off briskly, lifted into the dark
as the land-breeze variably puffs. Up above

searchlights find nothing but weather and themselves
(a dustier glare is where I see those headlamps

juddering for ever and all the way home
and hear the motor fire steadily) because

it's the end of the war, these are survivors
by the long wash of Australasian seas

a diminuendo of bells, guns, and prayers and
all these people simply enjoying themselves.

A wind freshens across the park, the crowd begins
thinning towards tomorrow. Climb up and see.

NARITA

Turning its eyes from side to side, inquiring
brightly, the head of the worm issues
from the door for arrivals.

The door for departures is where papers are
handed in. There are many of these,
all numbered. Never look back.

Between the two the meantime is all there is.
It passes of itself. Your cabin
crew girls are for off-duty

fantasies. Abaft the loo the tail section
ruptures, the sky inhales heavily,
a change of plan is announced,

all four hundred, some gifted or beautiful
or with greedy heirs, have to die now,
only to make sure of you

this instant sooner or later than you think.
The prettiest accessories, like
silk scarf, matching lipstick, badge

of rank are brightness fallen from the air, you
will never see it. The uniformed
personnel most pitiably

heaped, colours of daedal feathers, the smells of
burning, a ring'd finger, a baby's
foot bagged for the mortuary.

No, you will never see it. Wish yourself then
the best of Lucifer's luck. This indoors
world's roof is geodetic,

as good as any heaven, and better lit
than the broad daylight it simulates,
out of hearing of the rising

and the falling scream and sight of the nearest
numbered gate. Picture to yourself some
small green hills with ginkgo trees.

THE VESPIARY; A FABLE

Its thoughts are modular, they attach themselves
to the young tree, the soffit of the back porch,
a grey box with multiple apertures where

its visible business is with legs and wings
purposefully hesitant, the unseen venom
is contingent, the sting for later inquiry.

I write. Those writings which we now identify
doubtfully as such yield nothing. I transcribe
tapes of the period recovered from pack ice,

leaning hard on the crude systems in use today.
I construe gaps, blips, ambiguous phonemes
and learn that the day after the first confirmed

sightings country children were sent home early
from school, a pet goat found stung dead on its tether.
Townspeople who'd never heard of honey dew

ran out into the streets, crying and silent.
Unopposed meanwhile, our oceanic nation's
defences in traditional disrepair,

the feral Vespoidea victory in their grasp
thrust inland, seized ornamental trees, PVC
downpipes breeches of abandoned guns ditched

cars, open mouths, armpits, natural nests
of which the naturalness has taken centuries
issuing the safe side of history's mirror.

I write. The past itself encoded itself
known only to itself and is dead, and we
live in our different style. No one knows how

many millions perished while our two species
achieved symbiosis by selection, between
this beach and that mountain 'under Capricorn',

in an agon of orifices, host and guest,
legs, wings, damp secretions. Now the dark swarms, my
lips mumble words over the busy bodies.

I write. The bones of the last boatpeople from
the north and the west lay somewhere under the dunes
where dogs dug and we played. When I was a kid

that's what we said. The safest thing's to touch nothing
on the beach, the back of the cave, the riverbed,
never leave the nest in the bush, where you were born

and suckled. A mother's cry stings me in my
mind's ear stuck to the tape, another tongue trapped
in the dead of time, *Attention! les guêpes!*

THE PUG-MILL

At his age, he must know what it is
to have hands of clay and a child looking on.
A life by dug-out light under the hillside,
he has copied so often the one

thought baked in the bones of his wrist, there's
no obvious excuse for stopping now, so long
as there's a next there's no last. I am this child.
I watch Mr Prisk raise his left hand

eye-level (his own) as high as where
a bit of unweeded green light leaks beneath
a punky window-sash and pull on the rope's
knotted end. Up above in the sun

his horse hears the bell and stumbles out
of a doze into the collar and begins
orbiting the pug-mill, plods a muddy zodiac
which in its turn turns. Clotted clay buries

the workbench again. With palping palms
he stuffs his mould, that's one more circle squared, one
more brick the desert will keep. A contribution.
Its damp six faces sparkle dully

because of the sand which helps them slide
out whole into the system we inhabit here.
Is there anything outside? The hillside steepens
till baffled it stops, this way by blue

air that way by blue water, a third
which escapes between I'm running barefoot home
Corsair Bay, Flea Beach, pines of the town Domain
past the burned-out house with one dead brick

chimney standing. They are asking *Where-
ever have you been?* I tell them *Helping Mr Prisk.*

CONTINUUM

The moon rolls over the roof and falls behind
my house, and the moon does neither of these things,
I am talking about myself.

It's not possible to get off to sleep or
the subject or the planet, nor to think thoughts.
Better barefoot it out the front

door and lean from the porch across the privets
and the palms into the washed-out creation,
a dark place with two particular

bright clouds dusted (query) by the moon, one's mine
the other's an adversary, which may depend
on the wind, or something.

A long moment stretches, the next one is not
on time. Not unaccountably the chill of
the planking underfoot rises

in the throat, for its part the night sky empties
the whole of its contents down. Turn on a bare
heel, close the door behind

on the author, cringing demiurge, who picks up
his litter and his tools and paces me back
to bed, stealthily in step.

A TIME OF DAY

A small charge for admission. Believers only.
Who present their tickets where a five-
barred farm gate gapes on its chain

and will file on to the thinly grassed paddock.
Out of afternoon pearl-dipped light the
dung-green biplane descended

and will return later, and later, late as
already it is. We are all born
of cloud again, in a caul

of linen lashed to the air-frame of the age,
smelling of the scorched raw castor oil
nine whirling cylinders pelt

up-country-smelling senses with, narcotic
joyrides, these helmeted barnstormers
heavier scented than hay,

harnesses, horsepiss, fleeces, phosphates and milk
under the fingernails. I'm pulling at
my father's hand *Would the little*

boy for selling the tickets? One helmet smiles
bending over yes, please yes let me,
my father hesitates, I

pull and I don't let go. Neither does the soul
of the world, whatever that is, lose
hold of the load, the bare blue

mountains and things hauled into the time of day
up that steep sky deepening from sea-
level all the way west again,

this paddock, the weight of everything, these people
waiting to be saved, without whom there's
no show, stay in place for ever.

A hand under each arm I'm held, I'm lifted
up and over and into an open
cockpit *Contact!* Gnome-LeRhône

fires ninefold, the chocks kicked clear, my balaclava
knits old sweat and foul oil, where tomorrow
was encloses me now.

The Loop in Lone Kauri Road
(1986)

A RAISED VOICE

Let it be Sunday and the alp-high
summer gale gusting to fifty miles.

Windmills groan in disbelief, the giant
in the pulpit enjoys his own credible

scale, stands twelve feet 'clothed in fine linen'
visibly white from the waist up, all

inferior parts masked, as my father
ascends three steps, is cupped like an egg.

The pulpit floor's eye-level, I look
up, Gordon Brown looks up, my father

looks down at his notes and begins in the
name of the father and of the son

and of the holy ghost amen, a voice
that says Jess to my mother, heightened

three steps, to which add the sanctuary
rise, the subdued pile of the Axminster

runner. Panels of a pale-coloured wood
liturgically pointed assemble

to enclose and to elevate the voice:
is it soft *kahikatea*, so readily

riddled by the worm of the borer
beetle but ideal for butter-boxes

or heart *kauri*? the rape of the northern
bush left plenty for pulpits and pews.

Gordon Brown, grocery and general store,
before kneeling always pushes one

oily vessel up clear of his head, the
tin lampshade clashes, the pulley squeaks.

I'm looking up into my thought
of my father, my certainty, he'll

be safe, but what about me? What else?
A voice descends, feet scrape, we all

stand up. The scent my mother wears is
vera violetta. That can't be it.

MOULES À LA MARINIÈRE

It took the sun six hours to peel
the sea from the gut, black underwater
dries out grey underfoot, 'cleft for me'

to look down. The dull thought of drowning
ebbed with the flood, this orifice entices
wide open, gargling, warm at the lips.

Not all the way down. The deepest
secretions don't drain, still you can 'feel'
what's below the bottom of the tide,

knowing more than's good for you: seabed
rock wetted perpetually with spectral
colours, quotations lifted from

life into a stony text, epigraphies
remembering shot-silk offals, trapped
green weed, petrifying mauves,

muddy cysts, mucus, your own interior
furnishings, glands, genitalia
of the slit reef spilling seawards:

walls all scabby pink, sprayed-on starfish,
gluey limpets, linings of the gut which
swallowing a wave throws up an ocean,

it smells of your nature, sickishly.
Hold on tight, by one hand, stripping
off the mussels, quick! with the other

into the bag, don't count cut bleeding
fingers. The tide scrapes the bottom,
blinded and a bit fouled with sand

the slack of the swell drools, fills, empties,
refills, your jeans are sodden
to the crotch, that's wet enough, the bag's

heavy enough: do you really want more
mussels, old swimmer, do you need
more drowning lessons? Here it comes, one

ten-foot wave after another, it's
all yours now and it's up to you down
in the gut and the blind gut

in the wet of your eye gorging
moules à la marinière,
an enormous weight! Nothing to the

tonnages of water lightly climbing
your back. Picked off alive and
kicking in the rip, did you 'feel'

unaccountably unsurprised by
how natural it all is, in the end,
no problem, the arms and legs have only

to exercise the right allowed by law,
last words, the succinctest body-language.
You're innocent. The sea does the rest.

DO NOT TOUCH THE EXHIBITS

A gulp of sea air, the train
bites off a beach, re-enters the rock.
A window, a blind cathode, greyly reflects,
Plato sits opposite, his nose in a map.
Where you're going's never what you see

and what you saw, is that where you went?
Is there a reef with an angler on it
whose rod makes a twitching U?
Has he landed his fat silver-gilt
dorado, smack! on a pan in the mind?

Why can't I cut corners and have them?
Daylight chips in again, with cypresses,
olives, loquat (*nespola* the Japan
medlar, not the one you eat rotten,
the other sort, butter-yellow, sweet

embedding slippery outsize pips),
artichokes, the native littoral
cultivations, rivermouth litter,
punctured cans, plastic bottles,
and behind (supposedly) the weatherish

pink and chrome villas gingerly
seated, shutters to seaward,
the Ligurian blue, too much of it.
Or weathering the long cape
another fisherman whose limping

boat I'm overhauling? a file
of red and white Martini sunbrollies
wheels in, peels off, drops back.
A brace of NATO frigates present
unmuzzled guns, 'optional extras'.

Beachcombings, introjections,
best stuffing for tunnels. Venus
on her lee-shore *poco mosso*
paroled from the Uffizi, screwed
to the wall under the baggage rack,

space reserved in the mind, goes
where I go, my side of the glass
beneath which our family motto's pinned,
è pericoloso sporghersi
indelibly incised on steel.

Rapallo, London
1983

ON THE ROAD TO EREWHON

*The Author wishes it to be understood that Erewhon is pronounced
as a word of three syllables, all short – thus, E-re-whon.*

– Samuel Butler, preface to *Erewhon*, 1872.

Once past the icefalls and the teeth of
noon, already descending the pass,
out of a cloud blackened by lightning,
if mirrors can spell and maps don't lie,
that's the Erewhon road, the ambush

can't be far. Gigantic statues shock
you down to size. Before the Hyksos
their senate debated what's to be
done with you. They have mouths the mountain
blast vociferates in, a people

had need of these or these of themselves
were the need *causa sui*. Inhuman
syllables, harmony that howls and
hails, halting you. Patches of old snow
squeak underfoot. Goat-tracks, lost writings.

Six or seven times larger than life,
of great antiquity, worn and lichen
grown. They were ten in number . . . I saw
that their heads had been hollowed. Fear,
pain, hate, cruelty once chopped into stone

stare out again, each head *a sort of*
organ-pipe, so that their mouths should catch
the wind. Earthly, unaccompanied
voices empty wind into wind, mist
into mist, rock into rock, these ten

commandments. Eight of them still seated,
two had fallen. The God who thinks alou̇d's
the worst, your own shadow's a friendlier
fright. Physical, *superhumanly*
malevolent faces look back, too

hard for your nature to bear, only
the legs and how fast they can carry
you the hell out of here *as though one*
of them would rush after me and grip
me . . . If it were just one of those dreams

where running gets you nowhere! This is
the mirrored map, the Erewhon road,
where you came from is where you're going,
the hammers in the brain keep time with
feet pounding downhill, the rivers are

swollen in the mind's eye. Back there, in
the cloud the trumpeting heads perform
their own *Te Deum.* Panicky antiphons
die down in the blood. You can shiver
suddenly, for no reason at all.

I

Is the word 'adult'? Utamaro's engulfing
vulvas, deep thought! Füssli's girls muscling in, a
moist-handled glans, *shockingly indelicate,*

poor wretch! Flaxman said, *looking ineffably
modest,* one didn't blame the widow Füssli's
thrift, who stoked the kitchen range with them, making

sea-coal burn bluer. Was less at stake for Bruno
in Venice, incinerated, ineffably
for something ineffable? Ashes, in the end.

Stuff your pillow-book with metaphysics for
the best bedside read, it takes the place of what
takes place, pictures or *pensées,* the same thing.

The picture of the mind revives, our poet
noticed, and so do I. These agreeable
sensations moved over and made room for *sad*

perplexity, and back again, having once
orbited the earth. I re-enter, entering
you. The mind's too full of itself, to make sense

of Pascal or the creed of Saint Athanasius
damp and hot from the press, 'would you believe it?'
What does God smell of but the dust of hassocks,

wine, laundered linen, a creation of Patou
fingertipped behind the ears? Angel surrogates
shinny up and down the fire-escape, flapping

at bedroom and bathroom windows, all fingers
and feathers. She's too full and he's too busy to
notice much, only *gleams of half-extinguished*

thought, in the light of what takes place, no other
light really than these, which take the place of it.
A particular darkness forgets our visits.

II

What happened? What's happening? Somebody drew
a funny face on a big shell, BANG! you're dead
all of you, Ol' Bill ducks his helmet, it flies

past grinning, or bounces off a parapet.
In a serious oil-painting nobody gets
obscenely eviscerated, the war artist's

a dab hand at cosmetic bandaging, he
patches up with white, with a fine tip adds red
for the head-wounds, mostly in the scalp and brow,

the eyes of the wounded are forget-me-not
blue, gun-flashes vermilion, virginal pink
for the faces, like begonia blooms in shit

which is khaki *dunnest smoke*, old-masterly
murk *that my keen knife see not the wound it makes*
nor Heaven peep through. Heaven does. One painted

star blinks benignly. A child in the sun sees
it all in The Queen's Gift Book where Adam hides
because he is naked. My bank manager's

choice is a framed cauliflower cloud, the atoll
vertically blown up out of a silk-screen
ocean. Glass catches the light. Entering, I

turn it to the wall, unwilling to pre-empt
the untriggered fact, the picture in the mind,
the job in hand. Its relevance is obscure.

III

What's pain time? Your long wire, Alvin Lucier, sings
to the oscillator, end over end, glistens
in your darkened gallery. This is our midnight
ride in a wet gale banging the heads of the trees

together. Quartz watches don't keep it, humane
quackery knows what's quickest for capital
offenders, mortal inhalation, 'lethal
injection', make up your mind, how would you like

to die? In a flash, a puff, *an unconscionable
time a-dying* the king said or was said to have
said? Duration is public, the intensity
private, God's wink, a lifetime, a million years.

Where are we now? Between gulps of gas, that's twice
I've asked, this time he answers Saint Luke's, meaning
the supermarket not the church, I grunt back
gratefully, meaning neither, the hospital's

any minute now by pain time, a quick fix could
conveniently snap the wire, drop the dumb ends
in a puddle of terminal quiet, no
more random glistenings, no sound-images

whipped off the street. I want it stopped. Where are we?
The ambulance corners with a shrug, straightens,
windshield wipers egg-scramble headlights, greens, reds,
ambers, unquantifiable messes of wet

incandescences. Squatting, he holds the gas
bottle as steadily as he can. I lie
still too. The driver's shoulder's a dark function.
It's an 'essential service' we all perform,

Monday is beginning, Sunday's casualties
unloading still, full as a party balloon
with pain the mind bobs unserviceably while
somebody is brought in dead. I want my shot

and a couple of 50mg
indocid is all I'm getting if that's true
about the key to the cupboard where they keep
the morphine and the sister who comes on duty

at five, that's four hours more of this, the
bloody sheet keeps slipping off. You get the picture?
Amnesia, muse of deletions, cancellations
revives, revises pain, a ride in the dark.

LO THESE ARE PARTS OF HIS WAYS

and to make up my mind about God before
he makes up his about me put myself
in Wallace Stevens's place and
God wherever he pleases
and a precious pair of us that makes

two minds in two minds each about
the other or say four deadlines
in search of a Last Supper
r.s.v.p. time running out
no entry on the diary's blank last

fly life's dateless day
numinous yesses and noes making
minds up alters nothing materially
can you see God changing his or
being in more than one about

anybody's finally settling
for 'naturally' the right one like
in the event of malfunction aborting
the count-down? our recreation's
chess he's white and I'm black

the board expands infinitely
at an infinite speed like Pascal's point
with mirrors which mirror mirrors
behind each of us his lips think
in his native Russian one forefinger

pauses on a pawn's or a bishop's
bonnet when it lifts we both know
that move's for keeps operations
belong to control where celestial
software lisps eternal

zero-zeroes to the pacemaker
aorta *soft drum* the screen's bare
of digits all circuits locked *prepare to*
meet thy God have you an appointment?
belief hung in mid-mind between

the ethereal and the dustiest
answers let it hang! whose creature
whose creator to believe him into
existence or out of it? the heart
grows obsolete bottled protons

of an irrefutable *might*
majesty dominion and power poke
infernal noses into heavenly
business mutually assured
destruction keeps both of us guessing

demonstrable changes in the forms
of matter like fire-storms hanging
fire *Et O ces voix*
d'enfants chantant DIES IRAE
DIES ILLA exist in a mirror

a lifted forefinger for God's sake
whose? playing for keeps
my playmate's one unbelievably small
particle and who knows whose dust's
on fire in whose mind's eye?

GARE SNCF GARAVAN

The day doesn't come to the boil, it guards
a banked-up flame under a cool first light.
Madame tethers her Siamese to the doorway
of the Gare SNCF, the shadier side
of the tracks where we mustn't stray.

The tracks are bare, the pines don't stir, the haze
is international, Cap Martin is a thing
in the mind's eye of 'that eternal sea',
Bordighera just one more. Behind the doorway
of the sanctuary, something rings, Madame is

answering. I am questioning a blossom of
some nameless yellow creeper about the excitements
of life on a warm wall. Pussy is overweight,
so is Madame, but active, panties and *collants*
hang from an upper room, over the yard side

of the Gare, the seaward, shaded by the dark
eyelashes of the pines in a light that is not
explicit. Landward the Alpes Maritimes lean
scarily steep-to, by the Gare clock
I can relax, nobody's yet begun saying

'to the mountains, fall on us', only indistinct
voices drop from the lemon-gardens, the villas.
A frequent service. Madame emerges, bearing her
official baton, producing a train from Nice,
Italy's minutes away, an old-fashioned thought,

an old-fashioned iron expostulation of
wheels, fluttering doors, interrupts nothing.
So much at risk, a miracle that so much gets
taken care of. Madame picks up her cat from
the *quai* and cuddles it, conversing with friends.

Menton, London
1983

CANTO OF SIGNS WITHOUT WONDERS

I look where I'm going, it's the way
    yesterday's and the day before's clouds
    depict themselves over and over

an affluently planted skyline:
    the clouds lay the whitenesses on thick
    over the bluenesses. The impasto

is unsigned, there's a kind of an impression
    of lettering rapidly rubbed out
    before I can read, pasted over again

and rewritten, the name of a famous
    product, the thing that's everything,
    the sky being prime space, anyway

the most public part of this universe.
    Speculative thunder is noises,
    contused vapours, colours into which

my eyes walk: high-flown language, logo and
    sign of a brand of which 'the authors
    are in eternity', at least some

country we never trade with. My eyes
    walk a tight wire made fast to a cloud,
    securest anchorage, the weather

man's promise of 'settled conditions'.
    Underfoot, the pavement keeps falling
    away step by step where I'm about

to pass the pianist's open door
    some *chant sans paroles* escapes: his patched
    iron roof leaked, he spread a tarpaulin

over the Steinway: two of his cats
    stare from the shade of the hydrangea.
    The pavement is still falling, my eyes

walk not precisely stepping high across
        craters and cones, 'best parts' of our city:
        volcanic pustules green a thousand

years, and for a couple of lifetimes
        these people, yesterday's and the day
        before's people, as far as the bluest

dilations of clouds and seas and names
        to call islands by. Less and less time
        remains, they purify their private

pools, uncapping the vials which protect
        from viral enemies: the prudent
        set aside sums for depreciation,

each year sell off a wasting asset,
        c'est la vie. The painter is freshing
        up yesterday's clouds by interior

light, he cleans his brushes, drinks a mug
        of instant coffee. The rusted VW
        meditates my other car is a Rolls.

And as they walk, those two, side by side,
        his hand fondles the blueness of her
        jeans, her thready rondure and the stitched

name of Levi Strauss, below the patch
        seeking. She takes the hand. The sign is
        what the maker means. Much more than that

calls for an impossible presence
        of mind, I look where I'm going and
        that way they depict themselves, yes

that's all for today, my eyes wired
        to a system there, feet falling in turn
        on the pavement which is falling away,

unsigned whitenesses, unsigned bluenesses.

A SIGHT FOR SORE EYES

They wrap mountains round my eyes,
they say 'look' and it's all what they say
where the colour, that's another word is
deepest blue, and that's the colour of
the wind, blowing this way, warm and dry
coming from the mountains, visibly.

I have eyes in the back of my neck
too, the sun is mumbling the day's news
over my head. In so many words.
My morning bath was warm, out of a tap.
This garden is just one year younger
than I, 'girdled round' five years ago

with six-foot galvanised iron on
rimu posts, the sawn timber elsewhere
supports the Number 8 fencing wire
with one barbed strand, a little rusted.
The new vicarage is a 'bungalow',
the veranda faces north by west,

casements are fashionable magic
again, since the double-hung sash went
out, opening on the forms of pain, of
mumbled words, mountainously pronounced.
Too small to see over, I can thread
my line of vision through a nail-hole

in the iron. I give it a tug.
The mountains have shifted at their moorings,
shudder and heave clear. The biggest wind's
in that quarter, it loosens the snows,
the Green Road is under water, old
Mr and Mrs Troon in a boat

are 'taken out' repeated in a dream
of the Troons, the Troons! What have I done?
What are the Troons doing 'taken out'
in a boat in the dark up Green Road,
old and ugly and wet? The wind was
never so dry and warm or the smell

of sheep so sour or the dust so thick
in the macrocarpas. The mountains
are the colour of wind, the highway
north is a pillar of dust by day
half-blinding riders and dogs, westward
the river still rises. My mother

bathes my eyes with boracic, she ties
up torn dianthus, delphinium, phlox
wasted on the alluvium the storm-
waters have been scraping seaward since
the sun mumbled the first implanted
word. My mother grows it all from seed.

THE LOOP IN LONE KAURI ROAD

By the same road to the same
sea, in the same two minds,
to run the last mile blind or
save it for later. These
are not alternatives.

So difficult to concentrate! a powerful
breath to blow the sea back
and a powerful hand to haul it
in, without overbalancing.
Scolded for inattention,

depending on the wind, I know
a *rimu* from a *rewarewa*
by the leaf not 'coarsely serrate',
observant of the road roping
seaward in the rain forest.

A studied performance, the way
I direct my eyes, position
my head, 'look interested'.
Fine crystal, the man said,
you can tell by the weight,

the colour, the texture. The dog
steadies, places a healthy turd
on the exact spot. We like it
in the sun, it keeps our backs
warm, the watertables

dribble down the raw red cutting
the road binds, injured natures are
perfect in themselves. We liked it
at the movies when they nuked the city,
and suspended our disbelief

in doomsday, helping out the movie.
NEW YORK STATE jogs past me,
ribcage under the t-shirt stacked
with software, heart-muscle programmed
for the once round trip,

crosses my mind, by the bridge
at the bottom, the road over which
and the stream underneath are thoughts
quickly dismissed, as we double
back, pacing ourselves.

Concentrate! the hawk lifts off
heavily with an offal of silence.
Forget that, and how the helicopter
clapper-clawed the sea, fire-bucketing
the forest, the nested flame.

You Will Know When You Get There
(1982)

A RELIABLE SERVICE

The world can end any time
it likes, say, 10.50 am
of a bright winter Saturday,

that's when the *Bay Belle*
casts off, the diesels are picking
up step, the boatmaster leans

to the wheel, the white water
shoves Paihia jetty back.
Nobody aboard but the two of us.

Fifteen minutes to Russell
was once upon a time
before, say, 10.50 am.

The ketch slogging seaward
off Kororàreka Point,
the ensign arrested in

mid-flap, are printed and
pinned on a wall at the end
of the world. No lunch

over there either, the place
at the beach is closed. The *Bay
Belle* is painted bright

blue from stem to stern.
She lifts attentively. That
will be all, I suppose.

A TOUCH OF THE HAND

Look down the slope of the pavement
a couple of kilometres, to where it empties
its eyeful of the phantoms of passers-by

into mid-morning light which tops it up again
with downtown shadows. There has to be a city
down there and there is, and an 'arm of the sea',

a cloud to sprinkle the pavement, a wind
to toss your hair, otherwise your free hand
wouldn't brush it from your eyes, a welcome

touch of sincerity. As they pass down hill
away from you, their backs, and uphill towards you
their faces, the ages, the sexes, the ways

they are dressed, even one 'smile of recognition',
beg an assurance the malice of your mind
withholds. Look down, confess it's you or they:

so empty your eye and fill it again, with
the light, the shadow, the cloud, the other city,
the innocence of this being that it's the malice

of your mind must be the ingredient making
you possible, and the touch which brushes
the hair from your eyes on the slope of the pavement.

THE WEATHER IN TOHUNGA CRESCENT

It becomes 'unnaturally' calm
the moment you wonder who's going
to be first to ask what's happened
to the wind when did we last see

or watch for it animate the
bunched long-bladed heads
of the *ti* tree and all the dials
fidget in the sky and then it did

and we breathed again? The moment
comes when the bay at the bottom
of the street has been glassy a moment
too long the wind is in a bag

with drowned kittens god knows
when that was and which of us
will be first to say funny what's happened?
And it won't be a silly question

when it's your turn in the usual
chair to stare up into the cloud-cover
in which a single gull steeply
stalling dead-centred the hole

in a zero the stillest abeyance
and vanished into the morning's
expressionless waterface
'not a line on paper' your finger

pricks as if it might but won't
be lifted for something say switch
off the life support system of the
whole damned visible material

world quite calmly would that be
fair to the neighbours or the birds
other ideas? Seven oystercatchers
at a standstill a study in black

and red beaks all the better to
stab with are modelling for Audubon
mounted on sand in the frame of your
own choice with nothing to shift

the cloud around the morning could
easily be dead mirror to mouth
not the foggiest hope fluttering
the wind-surfer lies flat on the beach

failing actual wind a pressure from
that quarter north-east as it happens
and another pressure like time
squeezes the isthmus the world you

didn't switch off so that coolly
as you recline bare-armed looking
up the spongy firmament has begun
drizzling the paper's getting wet

put the pen down go indoors
the wind bloweth as it listeth or listeth
not there's evidently something
up there and the thing is the spirit

whistle for it wait for it
one moment the one that's one too
many is the glassiest calm an
'intimate question' for the asking.

YOU GET WHAT YOU PAY FOR

One more of those perfections
of still water with houses
growing like trees with trees dipped
in first light
                that pearl of a
cloud excited by sunrise
may or may not be priceless
fine weather is not what it
was and you pay more every
day yesterday's blue was of
a depth and a brilliance you
don't find now

                    rich eccentric
having wisely ingested
his cake has it too dying
among treasures the weather
troubles him very little
you too Ananias keep
back part of the price
                    it all
hangs by a breath from the south
you too pushing seventy
wishing the weather were here
to stay the morning's moment
free
        knowing that it is not.

A FELLOW BEING

                    I
How is it that the thought
occurs
        over again of not
being (myself that is being
not) Dr Rayner
            and that when
it does that same moment the thought
of being him
            he being
dead for one thing and in
the light of such darkness
a fellow being?
                The syllogism
bubbles like
            a fart in a bottle
all men (major term) are
mortal all
            doctors (minor term)
are men
        therefore all
doctors

divinity dentistry
laws letters sciences cats
horses Dr Faustus Dr
Syntax Dr Slop and Thomas
the angelic Dr are
                                    (were)
mortal alas
                    there's a stone
with four names on it press
clippings photographs the year was
1931
        therefore
as things stand in the 'poetry
of fact' he's dead enough and I'm
alive (enough)
                            the sillyolgism
says that makes two of us and
what are we going to do about
that
        sub specie
aeternitatis
                        Anyway the
thought occurs and it's a fact
'attested by'
                            the occurrence from
time
        to time.

                    II
A yellowing sunrise
heightens the cliff
deepens the sea
                    the
wink of a lizard's
eye ago
                that's eighty
years
            and we're young
and getting rich isn't
the answer we want

to get big
      'a big fish'
already the American
Dental Parlors with
46,000 pleased patients
nothing to the money
he married
            more of that
later
   what else did
the sun that comforts my
westward windows
offer
      to his gaze and
grasp?
      I've a use for
this valley
            the same one
what else did he 'see by the
dawn's early light'?
a rare and a dreadful
vegetation
            vast bole by
swollen bole
            a sickness
peculiar to the soil
of the island stuffed up
into the sky jamming the
exits to the world
valley and belly
tumoured
            a case of
gigantism
            (pathological)
bole by bole sheer as
Karnak
      oh skip it
said the old priest of Ammon
what's holy about Karekare
sheer's sheer in Egypt
we know our geometry
moon-rockets are bigger and

dildoes are smaller
refinery chimneys
aren't trees
            (repeat trees)
Dr Rayner looked north
with an eye to the uses of
surgery and the cost
of extraction
            measuring
the height of the ridge
                        made it
1000 feet and too
steep for a tramway but
by God I'll
            Timber!
We've come and we'll stay till
there's not a stick standing.

                        III
Agathis australis a lofty
massive
            massive! tree
100 ft. (30m.) high
sometimes far
higher with columnar
                        columnar!
trunk 3 – 10 ft. diam.
or even more
            more!
spreading head of great
branches geysers pumping
cloudy jets clouds forming
dissipating
            sap is rivers
pouring the wrong way
up
    up!
        always on the
boil fruit a hard ovoid or
globose cone which falls to

pieces
      when ripe scattering
compressed winged
                winged!
seeds
     a forest a throw
where the March sun thrust
and thudded among the great
branches
         till they came
and out there the sea's
full of fish and the myths all
dry on the beach

           IV
and this god guy
            see
cuts the dad god's balls off
be-cause the mum god
              see
gets mad the way he kicks these
kids around
        see and
all this blood'n spunk sloshed like
she been blocked by these guys
they reckon was gods
            see
and she's preg again this other
bunch of kids giants
          they reckon
and he chucked his dad's balls
in the sea and that's how this other
chick got born that's what wet
dreams is about
         all balls and
bloody great lumps of fat
'dya reckon
          a rust-pimpled
car clatters down the valley
surfboards lashed tight

                         the boys
balance beautifully
                     half-erect
riding the boards arabesquing
green bellies translucencies
another wave rides fills bursts
pours upward
                     dry on the beach
a 'mature female' reads the
Woman's Weekly snuggling
bare breasts in warm sand
scallop and *tuatua* shells
lie around
                     unoccupied.

                         V
The soul of F.J. Rayner incarnated
in Toronto graduated doctor
of dental surgery Chicago

and there one-fleshed a
meat-packer's heiress happy couple
'holidaying in Delaware Park N.Y.'

top-hat and redingote side by side
in a motorised sulky of the
period c. 1897 thereafter 'toured

the world' not excluding Auckland
New Zealand where the above
mentioned stone bears also and

only the names of 'his friends'
2 Moodabes 1 Cole 'remembering his
sterling qualities and great

kindness' the soul of the doctor
sits at his study desk it
wears a starched Edwardian collar

cuffs necktie and pin it is
looking straight at me with a look
of an expression arrested yes

'a straight face' generally speaking
success doesn't smile the soul
of the doctor is no exception

its hair parted a little to the side
its moustache is a seal's the right
hand closed not clenched the left

rested on the desk shows one
big ring its trousers are confident of
'covering the loins and legs'

a well-tailored imagination
is the mufti of the soul
of the doctor behind his left

shoulder the barque *Njord* loading
timber an antique telephone
squats at his elbow

Rayner speaking *Doctor* Rayner
long-distance to Wellington
the threaded voices

looping around lakes volcanoes
you can tell the Minister
he can cut it up for butcher's blocks

or toothpicks for all I care
that's my price for the finest
kauri in the colony I can ship it

to Sydney or Manila or the moon
for double the money the money
talking the soul's language

which sits as if spiked
upright on crossed buttocks
reminded that there's a pain

commoner and more mortal than
the toothache and a chair
perfectly designed for the purpose

of holding the soul in an erect
posture the way they will say
'the eyes follow you' and why

do the eyes do so? You can't
flap them off like flies you've
got to do better than that.

VI

Other ways of putting the same
thing an abstraction a sum
of money
        big deal

        £1,000 *Reward*
for any dentist practicing in Auckland today who
can prove that he is the Originator of Painless
Dentistry. We are Auckland's best and largest
dental Concern. ELECTRICITY USED IN
ALL DEPARTMENTS.
        ODONTUNDER
makes pulling and filling painless. We have pur-
chased the secret of its manufacture . . . we pull
more teeth positively painless than all other den-
tists. Our references are twelve thousand patients
a year. Call in the morning and have your bad
teeth out, and go home in the evening with new
ones, if necessary.
  We make our best set of teeth for £3 3s fitted
with our Patent Double Suction, which positively
stops dropping down.
     AMERICAN DENTAL PARLORS, Queen &
        Wellesley Sts., *Auckland*
         Dr. RAYNER

whom Eliot R. Davis nonpareil
colonial brewer hotelier racing
man high-class pig breeder could
'only say' he found

a most genial man and the cheeriest of company
at all times. A dentist by profession and an
extremely clever businessman with an immense
number of commercial interests. He had a huge
forest of kauri timber on the West Coast near the
Manukau Harbour, out of which he made a small
fortune.

mile after mile precipitously
rifted ranges the cliff-bottom
beaches Whatipu Karekare
Paratohi Rock waist deep offshore
Piha Anawhata
                    having told his
nephew/secretary Prouting who
told Dick Scott (historian) 20
years was too long to wait in a
pond the size of the U.S.A
to become a big fish in a pond
like New Zealand I could be big
right away if anything bothered me
I could just eat it
                    an abstraction
one thing becoming another
'kind of poem' not leaving the
thing intact
                    all those trees and
Ethel his wife a lyric in her own
right 'a very wealthy woman' having
'a financial interest in Universal
'Pictures Hollywood' the movies
hit Queen Street
                    an abstraction registered
as the Hippodrome Picture Company
and plenty more
                        'a splendid cook'
in the opinion of Eliot R.
recollecting Moose Lodge later Cole's
where the Queen slept
                        long after
and the doctor's well-equipped launch
The Moose for trolling the lapping lake
waters of Rotoiti

                      'the finest
grilled trout imaginable'
                              Ethel
whose money 'it was generally felt
he was turning to good account'
travelled much of the time in Europe and
the U.S.
              life being practical criticism
of the poetry of wealth
                              is unspoiled
Nature any use after all and
what are we doing here?
                      'unfortunately
in very bad health' she died
in Canada having left this country
not long before
                      date omitted.

                      VII
Late among the locusts
to the ripest crop
'columnar' Karekare
valleys to the north
late among the locusts
the saw-teeth shining
for the swollen centuries
the locusts hadn't yet
eaten
        seven years
a few million board-feet
later and the big seas
which skittled the beach
tramway one wild
king tide and the bank paid the
doctor what he said
he sold that mill to
the Government
                      having
the right friends clearing
£18,000

and £100,000
royalties the sterling
quality of the man
and
        why don't you send
the money to America
Fred? they said
Kaiser Bill's at the gates
of Paris anything can
happen
                no it can't
God won't let it and
built himself a statelier
mansion in Almorah
road Epsom Auckland
'magnificent view of the
harbour and landscape'
and there was *talk*
                        doesn't he
know there's a war on?
What about those flashing lights
from the windows pro-German
don't tell me von Luckner's
not watching
                prisoner of Motuihe
island
        and why's he got that
Turkish bath with mirrors
all round and the *electric*
light under the mirrors and the
doors between the bedrooms
hidden in the wardrobes?

                VIII
'lots of detractors the usual lot
of men who make good financially
or any other way' so Eliot R.

whose mum-in-law (1911) bought the
first Rolls-Royce seen in New Zealand

and who motored one day with the doctor
to Hamilton a hundred miles to the
music of boiling radiators
and exploding 'pneumatic' tyres

and who (Eliot R. that is) did
know there was a war on and sailed
to Sydney twice one month 'buying and

selling whisky in big quantities'
on which active service having been lucky
not to die pondered the all-wisdom of

the One who 'shapes our ends' ordaining
the *Wimmera* (poor Captain Kell)
must hit a mine and not the *Manuka*

preciously freighted with 'another batch
of whisky from the Americans' Charlie Macindoe
and not least if last Eliot R.

who lived 30 years more to put on record
appreciatively that the doctor 'a great
Bohemian always lived on the best'.

                        IX
The fatty fumes of Abels
margarine factory 'wafted'
on the north-easterly weather
heavy and warm this autumn
creep under low cloud-cover

up the affluently wooded
elevations of Almorah Road
the young executives and the
professional men understand
glossy pictures don't stink

the doctor's uplifted house
or home if that's the idea
is intact a stately shanty
by a World War I domestic
architect out of *Country Life*

in Hampstead it would've had more
knobs but if any fool's folly
ran to hallways two floors high
30ft long the wainscoting
wouldn't be Karekare *kauri*

stained rosewood colour or
the upper floors cladded
with weathering cedar shingles
and the shallow-pitched roof
so anxiously angled an

architecture of evasions
and asseverations *le style
c'est l'homme* Sir Carrick
Robertson 'prominent surgeon'
afterwards liked the outlook

over the trees the unedited
harbour views anybody's islands
a 'beautifully situated'
shabbiness too has its own
classical attributes

grubbiness its grandeurs under
the doctor's porte cochère
the latest cheesiest-lacquered
Japanese hatchback snuggles
long after half of the gardens

and the croquet lawn sliced
off in a storm of steel
pitched from the edge into the age
and the gorge of the motorway leaving
a house with nowhere to fall.

X

I might remember the year you
died but not for that reason
paths cross where nobody comes or
somebody's late it must have

been that in 1931
your soul could have dragged itself
as far as the dawn clifftop
over Anawhata or been torn

from death duties or been sucked
up and scaled off with the sea fog
or spilled into the creeks which drain
the steepnesses worming

its way the dragonflies and
the mosquitoes rise in their day
on wings of success humming
the way money hums and the saw-teeth

your life-cycle and mine
humming the hymn of it's finished
to the tune of it's just begun
fifty years 'later' the

questions open as the high-pitched
morning gapes to the sea
what was all the hurry? and who
on earth is that leaning into the

freshening westerly? *Agathis
australis* could've towered and
rotted in peace any number
of irrelevant centuries the year

I remember is the first I visited
the sun-drowning clifftop and
you died the two facts being
unconnected except I've come

where the paths cross the two of us
on collusion course the
'columnar' the elephant-limbed
conifers of this western

ocean toppled and rolled you
had only to lift your hand the
dank valleys delivered
shiploads ships houses theatres

railway cars the seeds are flying
down into the teeth of the wind
the bulldozers the week-end visitors
in March on my roof the bursting

cone wakes me like hail the soul
flies this way and that in the thinning
dawn dark where the paths cross and the
young trees know only how to grow.

AFTER DINNER
Arnold Wall 1869-1966

At ninety he told the press,
I suppose you are going to ask me
how I manage to live so long,
and so well.
        Five years later,
facing me across his table,
having lifted the glass of red
wine to an untremulous
lip, and set it down
with a steady hand, he remarked
that he once possessed the whole
of the *Comédie Humaine*
in a Paris edition. Couldn't
remember now what became of it.

Between him and his death's
left foot the gangrene was
no secret, already in the door
and pressing hard, in a white fold freshly
dressed for dinner.
                    Other whitenesses
were summits, mountain faces,
alps both Southern and Swiss,
Tibet, one icy toehold
after another, still climbing now
in the thinnest air, the last
of all those ups and downs.

Having read many books, taught some,
and written a few, after dinner
announced, as it were, a decision,
I have been here long enough.

A little after that, Lawrence?
D.H. Lawrence? Terrible young man.
Ran away with my friend Weekley's wife.

All true, as it happened. Twice
the mortifying foot, from under the table
published his pang, the grimace no sooner
read than cancelled, very civilly.

A PASSION FOR TRAVEL

Absently the proof-reader corrects
the typesetter. According to copy
the word is exotic. He cancels
the literal r and writes an x.

A word replaces a word. Discrepant
signs, absurd similitudes
touch one another, couple promiscuously.
He doesn't need Schopenhauer

to tell him only exceptional intellects
at exceptional moments ever get any
nearer than that, and when they do
it gives them one hell of a fright.

He's exercised, minding his exes and ars.
If Eros laughs, as the other philosopher
says, and if either word's a world
'offering plentiful material for humour',

that's not in copy. After dark,
that's when the fun starts, there's a room
thick with globes, testers, bell-pulls
rare fruits, painted and woven pictures,

pakeha thistles in the wrong forest,
at Palermo the palm lily *ti australis*
in the Botanical Gardens, Vincento
in white shorts trimming the red canoe

pulled the octopus inside out
like a sock, *Calamari!* The tall German
blonde wading beside, pudenda awash,
exquisitely shocked by a man's hands

doing so much so quickly,
Calamari! Those 'crystalline'
aeolian shallows lap the anemone
which puckers the bikini, her delicacy.

Short of an exceptional moment, if only
just! In his make-do world a word
replaces a white vapour, the sky
heightens by a stroke of the pen.

THE PARAKEETS AT KAREKARE

The feathers and the colours cry
on a high note which ricochets
off the monologue of the morning sun
the long winded sea, off Paratohi posturing
on a scene waiting to be painted.

Scarlet is a squawk, the green
yelps, yellow is the tightest cord
near snapping, the one high note, a sweet-sour
music not for listening. The end is
less than a step and a wink

away as the parakeet flies.
Darkness and a kind of silence under
the cliff cuts the performance,
a moment's mixture. Can scavenging
memory help itself?

What do I imagine coloured words
are for, and simple grammatical
realities like, 'I am walking to the beach'
and 'I have no idea what the sky can mean
by a twist of windy cloud'?

What's the distance between us all
as the rosella cries its tricolour
ricochet, the tacit cliff, Paratohi
Rock in bullbacked seas, my walking eye
and a twist of windy cloud?

DIALOGUE WITH FOUR ROCKS

I

High and heavy seas all the winter
dropped the floor of the beach the whole mile
exposing more rocks than anybody
imagined the biggest surprise a
reef the size of a visiting beast
you have to walk round
                                        a formation
out of the gut of the gales the noise
the haze the vocabulary of
water and wind
                            the thing 'demands an
answer'
            I know you do you know me?

the sea shovels away all that loose
land and shovels it back underfoot's
a ball of sand stitched together with
spun lupin and looping spinifex
making it look natural
                                    little
as you like to think nothing's either
covered or uncovered for ever.

II

A wall of human bone the size
of a small church isn't easy
to conceive
                neither is the rock
which overhangs me overhung
itself by cloud-cover cupping
the uproars of up-ended seas
and overhanging us all the
hot star which nothing overhangs

the wig it wears is trees knotted
by the prevailing westerlies
'chapleted' with clematis and
kowhai at this height of the spring's
infestations of white and gold
a cerebrum behind the bone
'thinking big'
                    proportionately
to the size of the thing
                         doesn't
have to be visible if it
stoops to speak so to speak the word
of a stony secret dislodged
the creator knows he's made it!
his mate matter
                out of nothing
a tied tongue loosed the stony ghost
before all of us talking all
at once in our own languages
the parakeet's brilliant remarks
the fluent silences of the
eel in the pool
                I think the rock
thinks and my thought is what it thinks.

                    III
A rock face is creased in
places in others cracked
through to itself I have

never climbed though children
sometimes do up to the
chin of the cave below

I always look up though
something else is always
uppermost a cloud scuds

past the sun reappears
yellow lichens ashy
patches thicken sicken

on the skin of the face
of the rock from spots the
size of the iris of a

mouse's eye to a smashed
egg the rock is wetted
by a weeping lesion

long after the rain stopped
it looks down I look up
a wink is sufficient.

                    IV
Memory is a stonier
place at the farm they called it
Rocky Gully blackberry
claws me back where I'm crawling

pistol-gripping the rifle
at arm's length after the hurt
hare my two bullets in its
body and couldn't reach it

where the third aimed blindly hit
home recesses of mother
rock overhang me and the
sun the rock offering no

choice of exit under the
one skin hare and hound I catch
myself listening for the shot
in the dark I shall not hear.

AN EXCELLENT MEMORY

Brasch wrote 'these islands' and I
'two islands' counting one short,
and 'the islands' in our language
were remoter, palmier Polynesian chartings,
a there for a here. The cartographer
dots them in, the depth of his blue
denotes the depth of the entirely
surrounding water. The natives,
given time, with the help of an atlas,
come to recognize in the features of
the coastline a face
of their own, a puzzled mirror
for a puzzling globe. 'Always in these
islands', that was Charles Brasch
getting it right the very first time.

Pat Laking knew it by heart the whole sonnet
all the way down to 'distance
looks our way' and it did,
over the martinis in Observatory Circle,
Washington D.C., demanding by way
of an answering look nothing more
than an excellent memory. That was
8 November 1974, just about
midnight, give or take a few minutes.

THE OCEAN IS A JAM JAR

Hearing my name in the barnsize bar
of the Tokomaru pub where you cross the road
and walk into the Pacific
Rua made me a small
comically deferential bow
spreading his hands as far
apart as they could go
'You are a *haapuka*!'

and I affecting modesty
comically flattered
flatteringly comic with
hands a bit closer together
'No not a *haapuka* a *kahawai*'

and Rua closing his hands
to the little fish size
perfect at this game
'Perhaps a *maomao*?'

a long way off in the city
in another sort of bar
one stuffed rainbow trout adorned
the wall and a mirror swimmingly
reflected the weed and the cloud
a jam jar full of tadpoles.

IMPROMPTU IN A LOW KEY

None of those was Eden
    I was as far
from that as from this, one's
    own personal
infancy of orchard
    grass grasshoppers
and a Black Prince apple
    or ten summers

later the long breath held
   bursting under-
water in Corsair Bay
   and breaking
surface from the deep green
   dive,
       the breathless
exhalation tweaking
   the neck, half-blind
fish snapping at sunlight.
   None of those was
anywhere near,
         neither was
   the summer come
of sex, give me a hand
   I'll take it.
Fifty onces and sinces,
   paradises
are statistics, I'm as
   far as *ever*,
the older one gets the
   better one gets
the hang of it all the
   essential
onceness.
       Visitors dig
other people's Edens
   there's a sign in
Sicily GROTTA DI
   POLIFEMO,
when you get there you see
   why Homer was
blind as a bat and the
   town football pitch
is netted all round with
   rusty wire.
Interesting,
       the way
the English say
round the corner and the
   Romans *cento*
metri.

          I'm a stranger
       here myself,
sorry,
          give me a hand.
    You heard what the
    man said, keep right on you
       can't miss it.

ORGANO AD LIBITUM

For beauty with her bande
These croked cares hath wrought,
And shipped me into the lande,
From which I first was brought.
          Thomas, Lord Vaux 1510-1556

                    I
Time's up you're got up to kill
the lilies and the ferns on wires
the brightwork the sorrowful silk
ribbons the cards the cars

the black twelve-legged beast
rises the dance begins
the six shoulders heave
you up the organist sits

with his back to you and your hobbling
pomp *largo* it says
e grave his fingers walk but
none of the feet is in step

he polishes the stool he rocks on
the bones of his arse he reaches
for a handful of stops he's nodding
yes to your proceeding

perched on a mountain with
'rows upon rows of pipes
set in cliffs and precipices'
growing and growing 'in a blaze

of brilliant light' that sort
of stuff is packaging
printed matter only if only
there were more to it than that

(shriek!) you could see 'his body
swaying from side to side amid the
storm of huge arpeggioed
harmonies crashing overhead'

in a cloud a bandaging whiteout
'his head buried forward towards
a keyboard' busier than God
and you that wool-shed sleeper

the one who saw in his dream
was it Handel high among the icefalls the
big wig nodding mountainously
swaying playing the instrument

had to be big enough to drown
Sam Butler's rivers up there in
Erewhon chapter IV and climbed
uselessly towards the source

of the music this isn't a dream
west of the main divide
Nowherewhon sounds no trumpets
this afternoon everyone present is

wide awake nobody's dreaming
least of all you (you) steady there
hang on *taihoa*! the organist's
fingers trot he breathes through

dusty curtains a husky
vox humana out of dusty
pipes fat candles for Sister
Cecilia's jig-time fingering

diddledy-dancing you down
hold tight there brother in the box
saying after me 'It was
no dreme: I lay brode waking' and

II

saying after me it was *raunchy*
and heavy with lilies in the chapel of
Walerian Borowczyk's blue (blue)
nunnery
      she leaned she fondled the
keyboard the pipes blew kisses
to the mouth her virgin sisters
dressed the altar-table dusted
the pews
      every one a beauty
(beauty) 'dangerous; does set danc-
ing blood' Fr Hopkins S.J.
specialist

      swaying she swept up
nympholept handfuls flung
on the bloodstream a sister playing
organo ad libitum jiggetty-jig on the
woodcutter's cock and the butcher's
block
      Paris having the rottenest
summer for years the crowds
packed in out of the rain to the
Cinéma Paramount leaving
Montparnasse to the web-footed tourists
and the taxis
      dead in her bed
by toxic additive smuggled and
slipped from the knickers to the coffee cup
the gaunt Mother lay
      and they danced
their hot pants down on the stony
gallery for joy of their nubility
crying 'La Mère est morte!' they

swung on the bellrope naked making the
bell-mouth boom at the sun
                              one
sneeze of the gusting equinox
whipped the doors from the bolts and up
went the scarlet skirts of the cardinal
dead leaves and fingers
                              flying
to the roaring organ the guffaw
of the daylight and the rain pouring
from the outside in
                              the movie's
over
          will you get up and go?

                    III
The organist blows his nose folds
his music switches the power off

getting into the 'waiting cars' they
postpone the politics of eternity

till time permits which is after the
cards the flowers the municipal

oil-fired furnace the hole
in the ground one after after

another thereafter before you
know where you are you were.

                    IV
No bookshelf in the room
                    the Gideons'
bible in the drawer the last occupant
never opened is a black book
lying in wait
               lucky you brought

your bedside paperbacks prismatic
blue green yellow purple
one celebrated psychiatric
teacher and there's this marvellous
meteorite or enormous
boulder of Magritte a motto for
Sisyphus beneath which you are that
prone figure folded in scarlet perfectly
composed exposed in a
window for anyone who cares to know
what it's like in these rooms for sleeping
off life
  'O Faustus lay that
damned book aside read read
the scriptures' watch out for the
fish-hooks in the small print

    V

     mark
the exits fasten your bible-belt
for take-off
   'the unlikely event
of an emergency'
     he sits with his
back to you 'busier than God' his
instrument flashes the crash is
programmed the music is magnified the
size of the side of an antarctic
volcano
   you disintegrate there
buzz buzz
   with or without your
loved ones and a face the mirror has
forgotten.

                    VI
          After is a car door
closing
          chlomp
a blinking light a wide gate
the main road
          chlomp
can I take you anywhere?

                    VII
Hands on the wheel and eyes on the road
reprieved into the time of day they notice
a yellow bus turning a tired female trundling

groceries 'belief in a hereafter'
wasn't so difficult was it? hardest of all
to believe what actually happens come to think

the difficulty was never to have believed
willingly in heat o'the sun or winter's rages
nor that here after all the hereafter hadn't much

going for it notwithstanding the beauty of
the language nor been listening
when the little dog said you can't eat it and you

can't fuck it sour grapes dogs having no
souls if you believe the books and what's
so special about you in your situation

apropos eating and fucking and
who writes the books? only men who do both or
if no-one did wouldn't exist.

palingenesis
        five syllables' worth
of pure vacation
          round trip
            returning
you don't know you've been
              born twice not again
'Fie upon such errors!
          To hear stuff of that
nature rends mine ears'
           Panurge said but Arthur
(Schopenhauer) three
           hundred years after
rather liked the thought
          looked forward to a
hereafter stocked with
          genuine spare parts
good as new nothing to
          burden the memory
naked on the beach
          now storms from the west
stand the sea on end
          it's an instrument
big enough to drown
          accompanies you
all the way down the
          'cold front' feathering
inland hanging its
          gauzes uncloses
closes teases you
          don't see anything
clearly
     taihoa!
          your replacement's on
his way
     you're naked
          as the fish bottled
'in its element'
          lifted to the sun
and it's the same wave
          spirits you away

out to sea while the
                    biodegradable
part picks up its heels
                    recycles all its
degradations
            fresh
                    wreaths every time and
no resurrections.

                    IX
                    The organist
locks up the console
                    Handel
booms at the sun
                    Tiziano's
rapt airborne virgin in the Frari
was an assumption removed *per*
restauro in '74 that too was a day of
sun wind and rain
                    Domenico's
mother said and he quoted 'life
is bitter we must sweeten the coffee'
shovelling the sugar
                    chlomp
'towards the source of the music'
                            chlomp
and they made the bell-mouth swing
swinging on the bell-rope
                    naked.

YOU WILL KNOW WHEN YOU GET THERE

Nobody comes up from the sea as late as this
in the day and the season, and nobody else goes down

the last steep kilometre, wet-metalled where
a shower passed shredding the light which keeps

pouring out of its tank in the sky, through summits,
trees, vapours thickening and thinning. Too

credibly by half celestial, the dammed
reservoir up there keeps emptying while the light lasts

over the sea, where it 'gathers the gold against
it'. The light is bits of crushed rock randomly

glinting underfoot, wetted by the short
shower, and down you go and so in its way does

the sun which gets there first. Boys, two of them,
turn campfirelit faces, a hesitancy to speak

is a hesitancy of the earth rolling back and away
behind this man going down to the sea with a bag

to pick mussels, having an arrangement with the tide,
the ocean to be shallowed three point seven metres,

one hour's light to be left and there's the excrescent
moon sponging off the last of it. A door

slams, a heavy wave, a door, the sea-floor shudders.
Down you go alone, so late, into the surge-black fissure.

An Incorrigible Music:
a sequence
(1979)

CANST THOU DRAW OUT LEVIATHAN WITH AN HOOK?

I

An old Green River knife had to be scraped
of blood rust, scales, the dulled edge scrubbed
with a stone to the decisive whisper of steel
on the lips of the wooden grip.

You now have a cloud in your hand
hung blue dark over the waves and edgewise
luminous, made fast by the two brass rivets
keeping body and blade together, leaving
the other thumb free for feeling
how the belly will be slit and the spine severed.

The big kahawai had to swim close
to the rocks which kicked at the waves
which kept on coming steeply steaming,
wave overhanging wave
in a strong to gale offshore wind.

The rocks kicked angrily, the rocks
hurt only themselves, the seas without a scratch
made out to be storming and shattering,
but it was all an act that they ever broke
into breakers or even secretively
raged like the rocks, the wreckage of the land,
the vertigo, the self-lacerating
hurt of the land.
                    Swimming closer
the kahawai drew down the steely cloud
and the lure, the line you cast
from cathedral rock, the thoughtful death
whispering to the thoughtless,

Will you be caught?

II

Never let them die of the air,
pick up your knife and drive it
through the gills with a twist,
let the blood run fast,
quick bleeding makes best eating.

III

An insult in the form of an apology
is the human answer to the inhuman
which rears up green roars down white,
and to the fish which is fearless:

if anyone knows a better it is a man
willing to abstain from his next breath,
who will not be found fishing from these rocks
but likeliest fished from the rip,

white belly to wetsuit black, swung copular
under the winching chopper's bubble,
too late for vomiting salt but fluent at last
in the languages of the sea.

IV

A rockpool catches the blood,
so that in a red cloud of itself
the kahawai lies white belly uppermost.

Scales will glue themselves to the rusting blade
of a cloud hand-uppermost in the rockpool.

V

Fingers and gobstick fail,
the hook's fast in the gullet,
the barb's behind the root
of the tongue and the tight
fibre is tearing the mouth
and you're caught, mate, you're caught,
the harder you pull it
the worse it hurts, and it makes
no sense whatever in the air
or the seas or the rocks
how you kick or cry, or sleeplessly
dream as you drown.

A big one! a big one!

A BALANCED BAIT IN HANDY PELLET FORM

Fluent in all the languages dead or living,
the sun comes up with a word of worlds all spinning
in a world of words, the way the mountain answers
to its name and that's the east and the sea *das meer,*
la mer, il mare Pacifico, and I am on my way to school

barefoot in frost beside the metalled road
which is beside the railway beside the water-race,
all spinning into the sun and all exorbitantly
expecting the one and identical, the concentric,
as the road, the rail, the water, and the bare feet run

eccentric to each other. Torlesse, no less,
first mountain capable of ice, joined the pursuit,
at its own pace revolved in a wintry blue
foot over summit, snow on each sunlit syllable,
taught speechless world-word word-world's ABC.

Because light is manifest by what it lights,
ladder-fern, fingernail, the dracophyllums
have these differing opacities, translucencies;
mown grass diversely parched is a skinned 'soul'
which the sun sloughed; similarly the spectral purples

perplexing the drab of the dugover topsoil
explain themselves too well to be understood.
There's no warmth here. The heart pulsates
to a tune of its own, and if unisons happen
how does anybody know? Dead snails

have left shells, trails, baffled epigraphy
and excreta of such slow short lives,
cut shorter by the pellets I 'scatter freely',
quick acting, eccentric to exorbitant flourishes
of shells, pencillings, drab or sunlit things

dead as you please, or as the other poet says,
Our life is a false nature 'tis not in
the harmony of things. There we go again, worrying
the concentric, the one and identical, to the bone
that's none of ours, eccentric to each other.

Millions die miserably never before their time.
The news comes late. Compassion sings to itself.
I read the excreta of all species, I write
a world as good as its word, active ingredient
30 g/kg (3%) Metaldehyde, in the form of a pellet.

IN THE DUOMO

I

Recitative

This is the rock where you cast your barbed wishes.
    That is the clifftop where you hang by the eyes.
    Here is where Leviathan lives.

It is all in the walls of one great shell incised.
    The instructions look simple, the trouble is the smoky
    ambiguous morning sunlight, the heights inside

the cathedral are blurred. So much for art, which only
    comprehends the introversions of arches,
    lunettes, capitals, where the sunlight slowly

floats up towards their rock-hung perches
    motes moths wings claws human hands fluttering
    prayers kites clapping gustily to barefoot beaches,

the tidiness of a carved by time discoloured
    eminence being magnetic to such poor untidy
    littles or nothings,

bits and pieces, yet 'of such' is the highly
    esteemed 'kingdom of heaven', what else?
    Imagine an enormous face, conceive it smiling

to an accompaniment of birds and bells
    down blurred clifftops, makebelieve masonry,
    by interior sunlight extinguished at eye level

which is rock bottom. Here the linens, the sacred
    silverware are arranged and the blood is poured
    by experienced hands which do not shake

serving up to Messer Domeneddio god and lord
    the recycled eternity of his butchered son,
    this mouthful of himself alive and warm.

This is homoousianus, this is the cup
    to catch and keep him in, this is where he floats
    in a red cloud of himself, this is morning sun

blotting the columns, the ogives, the hollowed throne,
    smoking the kite-high concavity of the cliff.
    This is the question, *Caught any fish?*
                      Say, *No.*

I am teaching Leviathan to swim.

A Professional Soldier

Ma ficca le occhi a valle che s'approccia
la riviera del sangue in la qual bolle
qual che per violenza in altrui noccia.

That's every one of us, man and woman and child.
We all boil together when we boil
up to our necks in the river so ardently imagined

(*Inferno* canto twelve lines 46-48),
merely to exist being even for the gentlest
the rape of another's breath or bread.

Gian-Battista Montesecco's problem was believing
everything he read, the divinest poets
told the sublimest lies, common sense was as rare

then as now, and that no such river existed
for stewing damned humanity was much too big
and flat a contradiction for this hired soldier,

throats cut, cities pillaged, assassinations,
no job too small, go anywhere. His theology
was eschatology, death judgment heaven hell,

he put last things first where they belong.
There's life to be got through yet eternity's only
a matter of time a hell of a long time.

Killer without qualms, he never forgot his basics,
they scared the daylights out of Montesecco
as nothing on earth could do, to do him justice.

III
A Turning Point in History

It had to be an offering acceptable
to God, for which good reason, and for others
of a practical nature they decided the cathedral
was the place, and the time High Mass.

The flood of a king tide, the deepest sounding
where the big ones are, the holiest lure,
the tackle secure, the steel and the stone
scraped crosswise *in hoc signo*, can you beat it?

Where the pavement is cold underfoot
and over it full flow, high blood, High Mass
brings purple and princelier scarlet
scuffing the sea floor, graining the green,

and the other poor fish and the drab
discolorations of plankton, il popolo del dio
threadbare in Tuscan shoddy, miraculous draught
in the visible and invisible nets.

Hot hand for the gold, he got cold feet,
Montesecco did. He told this fat cat Pazzi,
I'll do you a fair day's kill for a fair day's pay,
but the banquet's where we settled for, am I right?

You keep your side of it, I'll keep mine,
I'll dagger you a dozen Medici at anybody's table
except Christ's. Two will be sufficient, Pazzi said.
Who's paying? And Montesecco, Who's going to burn?

You can stuff the whole deal and to hell with the money
where it comes from. There's an Englishman down there
eternally boiling for chilling his man at Mass,
when they lifted up the Host he stuck in the steel.

A crick in the neck isn't the worst you get
staring at the judgment in the roof of San Giovanni
and the damned people the size of a skinned eel
in Beelzebub's teeth and the fire from Christ's left foot.

And you're caught, mate, you're caught!

I'll take my chance of the pit, Ser Jacopo,
but I'm waiting till I'm pushed if it's all the same,
I'm not jumping. To which Pazzi, What if I tell you
this is for Rome, the holy father himself

blesses the act? Not on for double the money,
Montesecco said. And might as logically say
another half chiliad later than this latest
photographer studying for Bonechi's *Guide*

Ghiberti's regilded doors of paradise
and the godsize Jesus dooming in the dome,
not counting the time eternity takes one day
mopping up the bloody mess on the floor below.

IV

26 April 1478

So they had to find somebody else
whose numinous nightmares
didn't unman his mind for the day's
churchmanlike chores,
whose mortal infirmities,
profane daydreams, dirt
in the ears and the nose, the involuntary
or surreptitious fart,

lascivious leakages,
the sea-cock under the cope,
were the daily wick, wax, oil and soot,
the smell of the shop,
for whom agnus and sursum corda
and gloria in excelsis,
candles on the lips, made light
of the darkest policies.

Pazzi found two priests
for the cathedral job,
Volterra's Antonio Maffei,
apostolic scribe,
Stefano curate of Montemurlo;
putting first things first,
whichever were last, they judged
the time right for murder.

Ite missa est.
The rite being said and done,
in a scarlet stir the hit-men edged
each to his man.
Lorenzo dropped his shoulder
quicker than Maffei struck
his fumbled blow and the blood ran down
from the nicked neck.

Blood fell, the rumpus rose
under the haughty summits
from the fractured glassy sea
to the mistiest limits,
and where was the other priest?
Stefano got no closer
than a dagger's draw from the mark
at the *ite missa*,

and the two young Cavalcanti
joined Il Magnifico,
and they knifed it out in the sacristy
to save Lorenzo,
leaving his brother dead
where he had to die
face down, by the Pazzi's jabbing steel
dancing wasp time.

Giuliano de' Medici
bled where he had to bleed,
bedrock flat on the church floor
in the cloud he made
of the strong bestial smell
of dissolving clay,
their offering to the oldest god
that holiest day.

V
An Old Hand

I tried from the cathedral
yesterday and had no luck,
Mrs Dragicevic said.

Slaty grey strata
angled and squared abutted
the clubfoot of the cliff

where she perched, this plump
vigilant bird, in her blue
quilted parka, pointing her

4.0 m. fibreglass pole
over each big wave that walked
white from the west

with a long bearded howl,
broke roaring into a run
for the rocks to come.

And the spot was a good one,
the cathedral, so long as you kept
your head for heights

and the big ones came,
il magnifico and his brothers
to the turn of the tide,

having to, having to come
leaping to the holy lure,
an acceptable offering

to the blooding hand, the scaling,
the scarlet clouded pool,
the necessary knife.

DICHTUNG UND WAHRHEIT

A man I know wrote a book about a man he knew
and this man, or so he the man I know said, fucked
and murdered a girl to save her from the others
who would have fucked and murdered this girl
much more painfully and without finer feelings,
for letting the Resistance down and herself be fucked
by officers of the army of occupation, an oblation
sweet-smelling to Mars and equally to porn god Priapus.

What a fucking shame, this man the one the man
I know knew decided, if you want a job done well
do it yourself, and he did and he left her in a bath
of blood from the hole in her neck which he carved
in soldierly fashion, a way we have in the commandos,
after the fuck he knew she didn't of course
was her last, and a far far better thing, wasn't it?
than the bloody fuckup it would have been if he'd left her
to be unzipped and jack-the-rippered by a bunch
of scabby patriots with no regimental pride.

And he had this idea, and he mopped up the mess
and he laid her out naked on a bed with a crucifix
round her neck for those bastards the others
the sods to find, furious it must have made them.
And the man I know who knew this man or some other
man who did never forget this fucking story,
it wouldn't leave him alone till he'd shown this goon
who actually did or said he did or was said to have done
the fucking deed what a better educated man
would have done and thought in his place.
And he wrote this book.

Experience like that, he exclaimed,
thrown away on a semiliterate whose English
was so imperfect you could hardly be certain
that what he did and what he said were connected,
let alone, by no fault of his own,

ignorant of the literature on the subject.
What can you do, with nothing but a cock
and a knife and a cuntful of cognac,
if you haven't got the talent?

A big one!

A COOL HEAD IN AN EMERGENCY

I

It will be back next minute
next week or tomorrow, if tonight
by the street lamp's negligence
it escapes, and the bells

yelling, the horns,
boots at the trot, motors racing,
doors wide with fright,
blotted faces looking

silly in an 'embarrassed
silence', the moment after,
will have been all about nothing.
No, not exactly all

or precisely nothing either,
but the word of a name escaped
custody, not even a man's or
absconding god's,

but the word of a name
scrawled by the roots of a tree
and the bole and the branch three-parts bare,
of what stood there

'in lawful custody',
escaped the cells and the rooms reserved
for the torturer's use, the mind's
painstaking hell.

II

The shock waves ringed, the shamefaced
street lamp reddened because
of what never should be but in truth
so commonly is

let slip to the dark,
where the tip of the tongue plays blind
man's buff and the wanted word
baffles the breath.

What's lawful here?
What's high or solid enough to keep
what's inside in? What's death
but a defect of memory?

III

It will be back, it will be
the beginning in the word, this *ginkgo*
safe in the cells, sludging the kerbstone
with colours of its fall,

frog's belly, canary's breast,
loquat or lemon or think of a thicker
yellow of a million mullioned glazes,
iridescences, buttered

sunlight. And think a little further,
up that street there's no necessity
to think anything at all, except of
an early winter gale,

the word of a name,
eyes in the usual places, the near side
of death's door daubed with autumnal redundancies
and verdurous chromatics.

BRING YOUR OWN VICTIM

I

For Isaac the ram,
    for Iphigeneia the goat,
under the knife in the nick
    was the substitute.

The rule was never to notice
    what had taken place
by the sea, in the thicket, the thing
    was your sacrifice.

Agamemnon didn't inquire
    nor did Abraham,
would the highest settle for a goat
    or oblige with a ram?

The heavens might be humane
    but you never knew,
you sharpened your knife, you did
    what they said to do.

II

History began to be true
    at a later time.
The gods got into the act
    and they played our game.

You killed your mother because
    they said you had to,
and before the agon was over you knew
    you must have been mad to.

Bring your own victim
    ruled from then on,
conscience cut its milk teeth
    on the live bone.

Brutus knew that the blood
        had to be Caesar's,
Caiaphas and Pilate found
        no proxy for Jesus.

You sharpened your knife, you steeled
        yourself, the wound
twisted the knife in the hand,
        the knife in the mind.

Man or beast you bought
        on the hoof hung dead,
neither the cloud nor the covert sun
        commented,

and you never knew
        what hung by the other hook
in the heart, your blessed sacrifice
        or your damned mistake.

                    III
You stood with an altar
        at your back, the grave
at your feet, no substitute offering
        to burn, wave, or heave.

You knew there was never nothing
        miracles wouldn't fix,
alone with your life, alone
        with your politics;

alive, alone, one-upping
        war, pestilence, famine,
happy in your Jonestowns, Hiroshimas,
        happy to be human,

happy to be history
        in a galaxy of your own
among the spitting and the shitting stars
        alive, alone.

Spillage of bird blood,
    fish, and flesh went,
the spoonful in the uterus, the aged
    and incontinent,

under your steeled thumb:
    so to imagine
slaughterman, overman, everyman,
    time's eminent surgeon.

THINGS TO DO WITH MOONLIGHT

I

Holy Week already and the moon
still gibbous, cutting it fine
for the full before Jesus rises,
and imaginably gold
and swollen in the humid heaven.

First, second, and last quarters
dated and done with now,
the moon pulls a face, a profane
extemporisation,
gold gibbous and loose on the night.

Hot cross buns were never like this,
the paschal configurations
and prefigurations could never have
nailed the moon down
to the bloody triangle on the hill.

By the spillage of light the sea told
the cliff precisely where to mark
the smallest hour when I woke
and went out to piss
thankfully, and thought of Descartes,

most thoughtful and doubtful pisser,
who between that humid light
and the dark of his mind discerned
nothing but his thoughts
e. & o.e. as credible, and himself

because he thought them, his body
had a soul, his soul had a body,
an altogether different matter,
and that made two of him
very singularly plural, *ergo*

sum couldn't be *sumus*. He thought
deeply and came up with the solution
of blood in spirit, holy adhesive,
God, singular sum
best bond for body and soul.

II

And the height of the night being humid,
thickened with autumn starlight
to the needed density and the sea
grumbling in the west,
something visceral took the shape of an idea,

a numen, a psyche, a soul,
a self, a cogitation squirmed
squirmed, somebody standing there
broke wind like a man
whose mind was on other things.

His back to me and black
against the gibbous gold
of the godless moon, still blinking
the liturgical full,
something stuck its ground like a man

in a posture of pissing out of doors,
thankfully by moonlight, thinking
of pissing, experiencing the pleasure
and the pleasure of thinking
of pissing, hearing also the sea's

habitual grumble. Descartes?
I queried, knowing perfectly well it was.
And he to me, Your Karekare doppelgänger
travesties me no worse
than the bodily tissue I sloughed in Stockholm –

no wonder I caught my death
teaching snow queen Christine,
surely as her midnights outglittered
my sharpest certainties
an icicle must pierce my lungs

(at five one midwinter morning,
the hour she appointed for philosophy
by frozen sea, freezing porches)
and my zeroed extension
wait there for the awful joyful thaw.

There's the customary stone I'm sure,
with the customary lie incised,
the truth being I exist here thinking,
this mild March night.
As for the thought, you're welcome.

III
No less true it was I, meaning me,
not he that was physically present
pissing, and metaphysically
minding the sepulchre
not to be opened till after the full moon.

Cogito. I borrowed his knife
to cut my throat and thoughtfully
saw the blood soaking the singular
gold humid night.
Ergo sum. Having relieved myself

of that small matter on my mind,
I leaned lighter on my pillow
for a gibbous moon, a philosopher's
finger on his cock,
and a comfortable grumble of the sea.

MORO ASSASSINATO

I

The Traveller

All the seas are one sea,
The blood one blood
and the hands one hand.

Ever is always today.
Time and again, the Tasman's
wrestler's shoulders

throw me on Karekare
beach, the obliterations
are one obliteration

of last year's Adriatic,
yesterday's Pacific,
the eyes are all one eye.

Paratohi rock, the bell-tower
of San Giorgio recompose
the mixture's moment;

the tales are all one tale
dead men tell, the minor
characters the living.

Nice and all as it was
and is, the dog-trotting sun
of early April nosing

the 'proud towers', to sit
at Nico's tables
on Zattere, and to watch

the Greek and the Russian ships
dead-slowing up the Giudecca
towards mainland Mestre's

raffineria, red-guttering
lanky steel candlestick:
nice and all the Chioggia

car-ferry making the long
wave wheelspoke from the bows,
slap-slop to the feet of the old

angler who trolls
past the Gesuati church, the pizzeria,
the house Ruskin lived in,

and to sit, deciphering
the morning's *Corriere*:
the lengthening anguish of

Eleonora, la Signora Moro,
now her fifth week begins
of unwidowed widowhood,

here and not here, to sit
by the sea which is all one,
where Paratohi is neither

steel stalk nor bell-tower
and either is Paratohi,
deciphering *Corriere*.

The tears of Eleonora
splash black, dry on the page,
the weather map, the fifth week

'after' the bloody abduction.
Ever remains today,
and the hands one hand.

II
An Urban Guerrilla

The real stress came from life in the group . . . we were
caught up in a game that to the present day I still don't fully
see through. – MICHAEL BAUMANN, 'MOST SOUGHT AFTER'
GERMAN TERRORIST

It was a feather of paint
in a corner of the window,
a thread hanging from the hem
of the curtain, it was

the transistor standing on the corner
of the fridge, the switches
on the transistor, the way they were placed
in a dead design, it was where
the table stood, it was the label
Grappa Julia on the bottle
not quite half empty,

the faces that came and went,
the seven of us comrades
like the days of the week repeating
themselves, themselves,
it was cleaning your gun ten times
a day, taking time
washing your cock, no love
lost, aimlessly fondling
the things that think faster than fingers,
trigger friggers, gunsuckers.
People said, Andreas Baader

'had an almost sexual relationship
with pistols', his favourite fuck
was a Heckler & Koch. Not that sex
wasn't free for all and in all
possible styles, but not all of us
or any of us all of the time –
while agreeing, in principle,
that any combination of abcdefg
encoded orgasm, X being any
given number – got our sums right.

Dust thickened on the mirror,
the once gay playmate,
on the dildo in the drawer,
dust on the file of newspapers;
silence as dusty as death
on the radio, nobody can hear
the police dragging their feet;
sometimes we squabbled, once
could have shot one another
in the dusty time, we had to be
terrible news, or die.

III
Lampoon

Nobody less than the biggest
    would do, and who was that?
Five times Prime Minister, the top
    Christian Democrat.
Two hours on his feet that day,
    talking the Catholics round
to live with the Communists' power
    in the parliament of the land:
President next of the butcher State,
    or the next to die
the death of an old crook, come at last
    to the reckoning day.

IV
16 March 1978

Normality was this car's
warm vinyl under the buttocks,
and the driver's nape,
the knuckles of his hand on the wheel,
the knowledge of exactly where
I was going, and why, and how,
point by point of my discourse,
A could be coaxed and B persuaded
and the State saved again.

Normality was the guns
worn close to the body of each
of the guards, good friends, composing
my escort sitting beside me,
and behind me the second car
completing the squad provided
by the Ministry of the Interior:
cheap at the price, when you think
of the Titians in the Borghese.

Normality was the moment's
mixture, moment by moment
improvising myself,
ideas, sensations, among them
the lacquered acridities
of ducted air in the car,
accelerations, decelerations,
nothing to be trusted further
than the mixture's moment.

Normality was no less
what it had to be, the ambush,
the crashed cars and the guards
gunned down dead in the street;
and the car that carried me next
here, to the dark classroom
of the Prison of the People.
Normality is, do you follow?
a condition very like mine.

The child I was would have known
better than the man I am,

when they tripped him, trapped him,
ripped his shirt, emptied his bag,

caught him, laughed him to tears,
rubbed cowshit into his hair,

the irreversible justice
of the wrong once done, the victim's

yes to the crime. Who knows
he had to be punished knows

how the women who wipe away
the tears and the shit

heal no hurt but their own.
Tell the bullet to climb

back up the barrel and close
the wound behind it. They carried me,

carrying the child who could teach me
my case was not so special.

V

The Prison of the People

Our household consisted
of, at a guess, half a dozen
comrades, both sexes, and a few
more, coming and going,

never forgetting one
supremely important person
for killing when the time came,
worth something alive

but how much, and for how long?
Understand, it was not a spacious
apartment, our elderly prisoner
had his own room;

the Prison of the People
was a tight squeeze, how long
would it take to squeeze the brain
till the fuses blew?

Not that we gave it a thought,
wasn't the State on the block
and the front page yelling rape,
and the cameras in at the fuck

and the dirtied pants scared off
the arses of the Bourses,
when we took him alive and we left
five dead in the street?

Not a thought. We slipped out for the papers,
read them ten times. We photographed
him, his shirt open, an unsmiling smile

on his lips, hung behind him the Red
Star banner and the words Brigate Rosse.
Christ! They printed it all. Next thing

we sentenced him to death. They printed this.
He wrote letters, we willingly accepted them
for delivery, Fanfani, Zaccagnini, Andreotti,

Cossiga, Dell'Andro, Eleonora his wife.
Did we seriously expect these would procure
the political deal, the exchange for our comrades

gaoled by the State, their liberty for his life?
'An episode in a war', terror for terror,
an honourable swap. So his letters argued.

He knew us better than they, adduced Palestinian
precedent, humane principle, the party interest,
all that shit. What did he, or we, expect?

Jesus wrote no letters to Judas or Caiaphas.
It was he or Barabbas, and that was another Rome.
Not known at this address. Try Simon Peter.

Silence in Jesus Square, his Demo-Christians
denied him by protocol, *il vero Moro è morto
il 16 Marzo, ultimo suo giorno di libertà.*

Consenting silence in the house of the Left,
Christ's communist other woman, three in a bed
with Rome, last word of his long clever speeches,

grosso orchestratore. And among themselves
read in his letters forgery, torture, drugs,
practices in the Prison of the People

which 30,000 police, etc., could never locate.
*Dead, by the party line, a just man we once knew,
of whose visible blood we shall be innocent.*

See ye to it.

       Can the same w.c.
receive the faeces of judge, executioner
and condemned man for 54 days,

in hearing of each other for 54 days
(and he, at an age to be father and grandfather,
with Jesuit's mastery of his Marx and his Mao,

knew us better than we knew ourselves)
and nobody be changed? 54 days
were the count-down, the Prison of the People

shrank like the ass's skin every time
the w.c. flushed, and we cleaned our guns,
and the newspapers yellowed, the execution

wouldn't wait, the silence outside
and the nothing more inside were the only orgasm
now, out of the barrel of a gun.

          VI
        The Letters

His letters. How can we know
who it is that speaks?
Covertly delivered by terrorist *postino*
to the press, *Messaggero, Vita, La Repubblica,*
from the Prison of the People,
so-called, an address unknown,
by what light were they written?
Under what drug? It is one
who writes with his hand, his signature,
la grafia sembra autentica.

True, I am a prisoner
and not in the best of spirits,
nevertheless believe me
this handwriting is mine,

so is the style.
Believe, do not speculate
about the effect of drugs,
my mind is clear, what I write I write
of my own will, uncoerced.

Get me out of this.

But I am, you would say,
not I but another who is not to be
taken seriously, not one word
in reply to my arguments.

My darling Noretta, After a little optimism,
fleeting and false, as it turns out, something
they said, I misunderstood, I see that the time
has come . . . no time to think
how incredible it is, this punishment
for my mildness and moderation . . . I have been wrong
all my life, meaning well, of course . . .
too late to change, nothing to do but admit
you were always right. What more can I say?
Only, could not some other way have been found to punish
us and our little ones? . . . I want one thing
to be clear, the entire responsibility
of the Demo-Christian Party by its absurd,
unbelievable conduct. Friends have done too little,
fearing for themselves perhaps . . . It has come
while hope hung by a thin thread, suddenly
and incomprehensibly, the order
for my execution . . . Sweetest Noretta,
I am in God's hands and yours. Pray for me.
Remember me tenderly, take our dear children
in your arms. God keep you all. I kiss you all.

(and writes) Monday, 24 April 1978,
newspaper *Vita* to Benigno Zaccagnini,
leader in extremis to party secretary.
I repeat, I do not accept
the unjust, ungrateful judgment of the party.
I absolve, I excuse nobody.

My cry is the cry of my family, wounded to death.
I request that at my funeral, nobody
representing the State, nor men of the Party,
take part, I ask to be followed by the few
who have truly wished me well and are therefore worthy
to go with me in their prayers, and in their love.

VII
The Executioners

Christ set it going and ascended,
leaving the engine running.

The R4 is a small popular car,
but a man could hunch himself

through the hatchback, the prisoner did,
as the guns instructed.

He looked his best that day,
thanks to the girl comrade

who washed and ironed his shirt
(by Ninarelli of Bologna, initialled A.M.),

the singlet and the long johns.
He took a shower, dressed himself,

knotted the blue necktie.
Only at the last moment I noticed

the socks were wrong-side out,
but the cars were ready by then.

A gesture with guns. Get in.
Silence was the last dignity possible

to the doubled-up foetus he made
in the baggage end of the R.4.

We shot him there and then,
the first of eleven bullets

clipped off the thumbnail of the left
hand raised by a stupid reflex

of the giant foetus in a dark blue
suit with cuffed trousers.

It squirmed, shrank, squirted red
and Gesù! he saw them

coming, the rods in our hands,
at one metre's range

the Beretta 7.65s
had to hit the left hunch-breast

eleven times, the grey head
whiplashed, nodding to the shots

yes yes yes yes
           yes yes yes
yes yes yes yes.

VIII
9 May 1978

Circumvesuviano is the railway
to Ercolano, Pompeii,
Torre Greco and other incubations
of Neapolitan poverty.
If you want ghosts for your money,
dig for yourself.

They are all dead as nineteen hundred
years or the moment after.
They do not live in memory or imagination
or history, or any other
of death's entertainments. Poems
don't work any more.

Back from a day among the ruins
to Piazza Garibaldi,
the Alfas, Fiats, Lancias, *tutto klaxon;*
the stone bonneted Liberator
rides nowhere any more and what's in a statue
but rocking-horse shit?

It is five in the afternoon.
Il Mattino, page one, X-nine columns,
Edizione Straordinaria,
MORO ASSASSINATO.
You're a guest, in a stricken house,
eavesdropper, easy tourist.

One of Rome's mediaeval gutters
is Via Caetani, near Jesus Square.
They parked the R4 with its riddled man.
You will visit the spot, there will be
mourners and flowers, many weeks,
both withered and fresh.

IX
The Poor

The poor publish their grief
on doors and doorways,

the black bar printed above
and below the name of the dead,

or needing no name,
per mio marito, mia moglie,

mio fratello, the scrap of newsprint
20 by 10 centimetres

pasted to the joinery in the masonry
centuries have nibbled,

the day's news, *Death was here.*
Dreamlessly nonna nods

into her ninetieth year,
where she sits, catching the sun

at the dark doorway;
over her, in black and white

run off at the *tipografia*
round the corner, which is always busy,

Per Aldo Moro

strikes off one more.

It ought to be impossible to be mistaken
about these herons, to begin with
you can count them, it's been done successfully
with swans daffodils blind mice, any number
of dead heroes and heavenly bodies.

Eleven herons are not baked in porcelain,
helpless to hatch the credulities of art
or to change places, e.g. number seven
counting from the left with number five,
or augment themselves by number twelve arriving
over the mangroves. Thirteen, fourteen, fifteen,
punctually the picture completes itself
and is never complete.

             The air
and the water being identically still,
each heron is four herons,
one right-side-up in the air,
one up-side-down in the tide,
and these two doubled by looking at.

The mudbacked mirrors in your head
multiply the possibilities of human
error, but what's the alternative?

The small wind instruments in the herons' throats
play an incorrigible music on a scale
incommensurate with hautboys and baroque wigs.

There's only one book in the world, and that's the one
everyone accurately misquotes.

A big one! A big one!

An Abominable Temper
(1973)

TO THE READER

Look for my fingerprints.
Good luck to you. I wore
no gloves when I burgled
your house and made off with
as much as I could carry,
a precious little. Now
I give myself up, what's in it
for you? All yours,

little as you knew or stared
or dreamt, the night I stole
in my stockinged face and feet,
shit-scared you'd wake and catch me,
when I whipped your skinny wallet,
your ten-dollar watch, pearls
of more pearliness than price.
You missed them, did you?

All losses are loss,
life itself the most trifling
some experts testify.
Hardly less precious, then,
to get your own back now,
a little, a little the worse
for wear, a restitution.
It's that, or nothing.

A WINDOW FRAME

I

This paper is eleven and three-quarter
inches long, eight and one-quarter inches
wide, this table four feet five inches long,
thirty-two inches wide, this room

twelve feet square, this house one
thousand square feet, this window encloses
two leafless peach branches on which I count
fifty twigs and then give up, one mile

away the morning sunlight whitens or darkens
what I take to be the walls of houses
and the roofs along a long ridge of the land.
I should be used to it by now, the refusal

to move an inch closer, an inch to the right
or left or (so long as I look) to dismantle
the hallucination of fact, the refusal even
to speak, to explain, as if it were unpardonable

mortal sin on my part not to have remembered.
Am I to burn in my chair for no worse fault
than pulling out the plug? Am I to bear
an eternal blame because the Pacific Ocean

disappeared down the pipe and sucked the sky
down with it? The edges of this sheet
of paper are beginning to brown, slightly,
but there is no definable smell of burning

in this house, this room. This window encloses
two leafless peach branches on which I count
fifty twigs and then give up. It will be the
fifty-first on which a sparrow settles,

cock sparrow, he picks under each wing
distinctly, so many times for the left,
so many for the right, one loses count.
He is not there now nor will be yet.

I should be used to it, the way numbers
won't go by numbers, the injustice of it
that finds me guilty. A sparrow has not fallen
to the ground. Do you smell burning?

It is not what you say,
it is not the way you say it,
it is not words in a certain order.

Look out the window.
                    It is on the page.
Examine the page.
                    It is out the window.
Knuckle the cool pane.
                    It is in the bone.
Why is the mud glassed,
                    with mangroves
bedded in the glass?
                    Why is the cloud
inverted in the glass?
                    Why are islands
in the Gulf stained blue
                    grained green with
interior lighting
                    by Hoyte?
                              Why not?

TO AN UNFORTUNATE YOUNG LADY WHO AFTER ATTENDING SIX PUBLIC READINGS BY THIRTY POETS ASKED, DOES ANYONE CARE?

How right you are, my dear,
Let us make an example of poetry.
It is possible, even for poets,
to live without it, so many do,
and to live with it, most of the time
impossible.
            Isn't it the rumble
of something loose behind,
or a fumble
in the back seat of the mind?
Or an innumerable company

of the heavenly host crying
rhubarb rhubarb rhubarb rhubarb
with obbligato innumerable other
syllables in several languages,
some dead?
            Does anyone care?
One man's rhubarb is another man's
artichoke and that's the reason why
the poetry of earth is never dead
dead dead.
            Rhubarb to you,
my dear, with cornflakes and cream,
every glorious carefree day and night of your life.

THIS BEACH CAN BE DANGEROUS

*The fatalities of his nature cannot be disentangled from the
    fatality of all that which has been and will be.*
                                        NIETZSCHE

WARNING
They came back, a well known face
familiarly transfigured, lifelikeness only
cancer, coronary, burning, mutilation
could have bestowed, they came by millions
and a friend or two calling me by my name
and my father, by a name no other could know.

BATHE BETWEEN THE FLAGS
Each with the same expression, his own,
mirrored in the sand or the mind, came back
the way they went calling like winter waves
pick-a-back on the humped horizon they rode
the strong disturbed westerly airstream
which covered the North Island.

DO NOT BATHE ALONE
It was their company that made it possible
for me to walk there, cracking the odd shell
with the butt of a manuka stick,
happy to the point of hopelessness.

TO DOUGLAS LILBURN AT FIFTY

My fiftieth year had come and gone. So Yeats,
in the course of one astonishing poem,
letting the fact drop, his timing perfect.

Toothless warriors, nonagenarian burgesses,
mumble the sweet cake, the spittled crumbs.
Somebody will blow out all the candles.

If you had your way, would you compose a score
with fifty bass drums gunning the day down
in self-salute? What do we expect?

A poor look-out for honest pastrycooks,
all the same, for the economy generally.
Come on, be a quinquagenarian!

It is only for one day. No two are alike.
Each has its singular fascination.
You are fifty only once.

The lightest of touches on the shoulder, this
unreckonable reminder, will it alter
the weather even a shade?

The written score affirms
shades, alterations, novelties,
the days and the midnights between the days:

in part, you will be persuaded to allow,
the music affirms, makes room at least
for silence to loom in

larger than in the hills where it first harboured,
eavesdropped upon, spied upon.
The idea was never to break it!

Is it fiddlers' armpit sweat, the punished
bellies of drums, bespittled brass,
cock-pitted against silence?

Is it bloodbeat, waterdrop, all manner alchemical
electronic tinctures? *'Tis magic,*
Magic that hath ravish'd me!

Hang up blonde promontories, MacDiarmid's oils.
Take down my book, some poet's attitude.
Set a silence to catch a silence.

Eavesdropper, what are you overhearing now?
Blow out the candles. Praise the cake.
Indulge the birthday guest.

1965

WHAT WAS THAT?

Now I heard in my dream
    or dreamt I heard
        the Last Trump
           it was not loud
seraphic brass
    made nobody jump
        sing glory glory
           or the damned scream

it was not loud
    more of a hum
        than a vocal murmur
           a unison
without voices
    no star performer
        blowing up the graveyards
           tooting on a cloud

it was the single sound of
all our deaths
unison of our last
confusion
stopped breaths
unison without blast
or lambsblood bath
world without end

Socrates died so
willingly Jesus
not without a struggle
gave up the ghost
and a mother pleases
to smother her baby
in the Bronx or the Urewera
some other pillow

brain-tissue splashed
fractionally after
the bullet-hole appeared
in the gib board
freesias and catheters
perfumed the ward
in a hospice for the dying
the Boeing crashed

the Trump played on
like a sea in my sleep
or the thumb-stopped ear
where my blood can listen
to the river of itself
nobody rose calling
deep to our deep
last unison.

A REFUSAL TO READ POEMS OF JAMES K. BAXTER AT A PERFORMANCE TO HONOUR HIS MEMORY IN CRANMER SQUARE, CHRISTCHURCH

Jim, you won't mind, will you,
if I don't come to your party?
One death is enough, I won't kill you
over again, ritually,
being only one other poet
who knew you younger and never better,
I would hardly know under which hat or which crown
to salute you now –
bays, or myrtles, or thorns,
or which of them best adorns
that grave ambiguous brow.

The quandary's mine, yours too,
Jim, isn't there always too much
we don't understand, too much that we do?
Winged words need no crutch,
and I've none for you.

March, 1973

TANTALUS

Tantalus, Tantalus, how are you getting on,
up to your guilty neck in the black river,
nothing to drink or to eat for an ever gone
and an ever to be?
                        Tantalus,
pick yourself a plum.
                        Tantalus,
dip your chin, drink.
                        Tantalus,
what's wrong with you?
                                    God,
he's hopeless!
            Tantalus!

AN ABOMINABLE TEMPER

H.A.H. Monro, 1814-1908, sometime Judge of the
Native Land Court, New Zealand, writes to his daughter,
Ada Morrison.

I

What little do I know?
Really very little indeed.
You suggest that I write it down.
Well, Ada, I shall try.
As much as I remember,
having forgotten the most.

We, whoever we are,
have seen the century out.
So conveniently, I might
have gone, that hundredth Hogmanay.
Raw 1901
is a socket my tongue touches

unhopefully. I take up my pen,
not without a little pain.
A hard frost again this morning,
a sharp frost, needle to the bone
as I crook my knuckle to the pen,
a black frost. I dip and scratch
like an old fowl. Winter

comes last for us all.
A fogged window, the gaslight
fizzing in the afternoon –
I feel the steel nib searching
skull bone, wrist bone.
Having forgotten the most,
dear Ada, I am writing it down,

the little of what I was told
by my father and my mother,
by this last light in my mind,
blue bead on a black wick,
which leaves most things dark.
I think my grandfather was killed

in a sea battle. Trafalgar?
Why not, if it suits you?
Any other battle would do.
This winter light's too dim
for embroidering by,
supposing I had the talent.

II

I am writing it down, as you say,
for my children and grandchildren,
or to oblige you, Ada.
I dip, and scratch.
What judgements did I scratch?
What claims? Whose lands?

Maori lands, when I was judge?
I am writing about my father.
He had an abominable temper –
That's written now.
When only a small boy,
he was taken to sea by his father,

the naval officer, who hoped
for a son in the same service.
In fact, he detested it.
I've often said, no wonder,
if the father and son were cursed
with the same bad temper.

Did my father hate his father
for a temper like his own?
No love was lost between him
and the sea, I'm sure of that.
I've often said, that first
voyage might have been his last –

I would not be sitting, Ada,
in this cold small city,
drizzling my winter away
out of the blinding mountains
into the blinded sea,
where the English trees don't care

what hemisphere this is
or month of the year,
and a hundred years are too
many, and too few.
I am writing about my father.
Quite a young man, he obtained

in his native Edinburgh,
some government situation.
I forget what, precisely.
I conclude it had a connexion
with the French wars, at all events
Waterloo was the end of it.
Othello's occupation was gone.

He could have had cash compensation
for the lost employment, or
he could name any colony for
his grant of land. The climate
in Tasmania was said to be healthy.
He sailed in the *Minerva*.

III

Six months at sea, with my mother,
my brother William, my sister
Marie – *tempestuous*.
I write down the one word
I ever heard of it.
I am sure, well chosen. It can hardly
have improved my father's temper.

But how promising it looked,
that Hobart landing!
Grass to the backs of the cattle
on the block my father chose.
It was her life's regret,
my mother would often say,

some blundering Sydney office
gave 400 trumpery acres,
Robinson's to my father,
and his fine block to Robinson.
Greener than the grass, my father
abandoned his rightful claim,

took money and lost a fortune.
He gained, in spite of it all,
a friend, Lieutenant Gunn,
ex-Imperial Army,
six foot six in his socks,
Commandant of Birch's Bay
convict station. Gunn

made me his special pet,
danced me on his knee.
A bushranger shot his arm off.
My father had his post,
with convict servants and all,
an eight-oared gig on the Derwent,
and a home rent free,

till the timber trade failed.
My father sailed
his own twenty-ton cutter
over to New Zealand.
Hell upon earth he found
at the Bay of Islands.
Hokianga, on the contrary,
agreeably surprised him,

the Maori a better class,
and so were the settlers,
several of them retired
army and naval officers,
highly respectable people
residing at Hokianga.

IV

My father found a purchaser there
for the twenty-ton cutter,
Count Dillon, a British sea-captain,
who obtained his title of Count
from a grateful French Government
for some service or other connected

with the mystery of La Pérouse's
expedition. Just what, precisely,
escapes me. He was a Count,
a reward, I am sure, as gratifying
to him, as it was inexpensive
to France. Back again to Hobart

my father sailed in a trading schooner,
chartered the brig *Brazil Packet*,
captain and crew, took us all aboard
for New Zealand. So far, dear Ada,
so near, perhaps I should say,
I have picked my thread for you,

my child, my other children,
your children, their children,
great-grandchildren of mine,
among others, Arnold, John, Allen,
great-great-grandsons Wystan, Timothy, Simon.
I dip, and scratch the hyphens,

not without a little pain
the steel nib searches
wrist bone, skull bone,
testicles, time stitches
hyphen by hyphen this hand-me-down
garment we wear in our turn,

shrunk in the wash, or threadbare.
I am twitched from behind
as I crook my knuckle to the pen.
I am writing about my father.
Peace to his loins, dust somewhere now
in San Francisco. The last voyage,
of which I write nothing.

V

A mouth made mountainous with mere sand
if ever dung yellow dunes were mountains
opened that morning to suck our ship in.

Out of many inlets, branches, root-breathers
of mangroves intaking, expelling pungent air,
a little strong for my taste now, not then,

mucus of a strange mother smeared us over
from head to foot. We were less visitors there
than visceral as hydatid worm to host.

Underfoot at Horeke the ground swayed civilly,
steadied, at the suggestion of our steps.
We lugged our worldly goods ashore,

   item tables and chairs
   item window sashes and doors (2)
   item bricks for the chimneys
   item one ton of flour
   item a team of four bullocks (£100)
   item a cart
   item a plough
   item harrows

On a block of land bought from the natives
the erection of a dwelling-house proceeded,
my mother, my two sisters and I meanwhile

accommodated in the house of a settler.
No sooner built than burned to the ground,
all our possessions with it. An accident,

at least I never heard anyone blamed for it.
My mother and sisters stayed on with the settler,
my father and I, my brother, our boy interpreter

(till more supplies could be obtained from Hobart)
roughed it in a hut the Maoris built for us,
one room, provided with

item one frying-pan
item four halves of coconut shell for cups
item mussel shells stuck on reeds for spoons

Clearing the land went on, a hundred Maoris
were employed on this. If I remember rightly,
the daily wage was half a fig of tobacco –

eighteen figs to the pound, sixpence per pound.
Labour was not dear in those days.
Not that as a child that would have occurred to me.

Burned to the ground, a smouldering heap
heaves into memory, he and his household goods,
cold ashes now. This charred fag-end of me

pokes here and there. All fires are accidents,
if one happens to be ninety years of age,
most accidents have done, as we say they will.

VI

Re-supplied from Hobart, my father had built
a large weatherboard house, outhouses, boatshed.
He enclosed several acres and made a garden.

Like the Garden of Eden, I am tempted to say.
If it had been less like – indeed, dear Ada,
you know your Bible, I hope, as well as I do.

Yes, it was a pleasant life at Hokianga,
only for my father's abominable temper
we could have been very happy,

with a hundred head of cattle, as many goats,
innumerable pigs, fowls, geese, ducks, turkeys,
a beautiful six-oared gig rowed by six Maoris

(boys, we called those in our regular employ)
and the shooting and fishing. My father kept
his bad temper entirely for home consumption,

149   *An Abominable Temper*

outside his family he never quarrelled with anyone.
The bad times came, the garden went
the way of all gardens from the first, I suppose.

Depression swept the Colonies,
Australia bankrupt, New Zealand fallen to zero.
Sails were few and listless on the Hokianga.

Disobedient to my father,
the timber trade failed again, the Maoris felled
no more kauri to make him spars for Chile.

Heke took an axe to the Flagstaff instead,
at the Bay of Islands. The War in the North began.
My father chartered a ship, the barque *Bolina*,

to carry us all, with his other belongings,
including the hundred cattle, south to Auckland.
I grew to manhood, married, you and the rest

came into the world. I write nothing of that.
Last light leaves most things dark, the nearer
the darker. Our secrets keep themselves.

VII

Did he love nobody?
Nobody him? Dear Ada,
I do not imagine my father
got me in a fit of temper,
whatever the connexion was.
Such things, if possible at all,
one prefers to think unlikely.

Can you, yourself, imagine
what the feeling was, my feeling
when my semen left me lonely
and you lonelier?
An absurd question. Precisely,
or I should not ask it.

Ask God why he does such things.

VIII

Was he of a romantic disposition?
Peter I mean, my father.
Born the same year as Keats
who shuddered at the sight of old women,
horrors! they knew too much,
and peppered his tongue
to taste the claret better,
I am sure he was otherwise preoccupied
in his native Edinburgh.

Was it smelly between the sheets?

What in the name of God and Robbie Burns
and the nine merry Muses was he doing
at Hokianga, not caring half a fig
of tobacco while the timber was profitable,
he with his gentlemanly tastes,
and the better class he never quarrelled with,
cherishing besides

> *item* one pair brass-barrelled black-nippled
> spring-daggered percussion duelling pistols
> *item* one *Poems* of Robert Burns, Edinburgh,
> 1812
> *item* one Holy Bible?

IX

My mother's maiden name was Alcock,
granddaughter of an Englishman.
County family. It took his butler
all day to clean the silver plate.
He in his dotage left the estate
to some other relative.

This fool
of a grandmother of mine! My mother
was robbed, the second time, of a fortune.

My mother's younger sister Jane
died, unmarried, long, long ago.

In the beginning was the four letter Word
Tetragrammaton, an angry father.
The pistols will be sold for fifty pounds
by my grandson Tremayne to Arthur Morten,
collector of old firearms, whose collection
will pass on his death to the Canterbury Museum,
Christchurch, New Zealand.
Allen will get the Bible and the *Poems*.

I speak as a fool, fools shall repeat after me.

This prophecy Allen *shall make,*
for I live before his time.

Trees, Effigies, Moving Objects
a sequence
(1972)

The first time I looked seaward, westward
it was looking back yellowly,
a dulling incandescence of the eye of day.
It was looking back over its raised hand.
Everything was backing away.

Read for a bit. It squinted between the lines.
Pages were backing away.
Print was busy with what print does,
trees with what trees do that time of day,
sun with what sun does, the sea
with one voice only, its own,
spoke no other language than that one.

There wasn't any track from which to hang
the black transparency that was travelling
south-away to the cold pole. It was cloud
browed over the yellow cornea which I called
an eyeball for want of another notion,
cloud above an ocean. It leaked.

Baldachin, black umbrella, bucket with a hole,
drizzled horizon, sleazy drape,
it hardly mattered which, or as much
what cometing bitchcraft, rocketed shitbags,
charred cherubim pocked and pitted the iceface
of space in time, the black traveller.
Everything was backing away.

The next time I looked seaward,
it was looking sooted red, a bloodshot cornea
browed with a shade that could be simulated
if the paint were thick enough, and audible,
to blow the coned noses of the young kauri,
the kettle spout sweating,
the hound snoring at my feet,
the taste of tobacco, the tacky fingers
on the pen, the paper from whose plane
the last time I looked seaward
would it be a mile, as the dust flies,

down the dulling valley, westward?
everything was backing away.

II FRIENDSHIP HEIGHTS

By night by fishes' light
I am absently walking in another summer,
a stranger here myself. The streetlamps
and the headlamps hang and swim in waves
greened round, quite extraordinarily like
a fish-tank forest. Presently I shall see
deep avenues there, extraordinarily like
a neighbourhood called Friendship, another time.

On the sidewalk an iron receptacle
NOT FOR THE DEPOSIT OF MAIL.
This other one is the right one
FOR U.S. MAIL, the hollow lovers' tree
black as a thought of the world inside.

Receptacle, receive me, receive me.

Each cave is calm as if no traffic stormed,
the six-lane fugue is lost on the deaf leaf.
Cave, storm, fugue, forest could be very like
a neighbourhood called Friendship: only semblances
are lost on the black hollow iron tree
and the deaf leaf gurgles to itself by night
by fishes' light. Another semblance might
be absently walking, in another summer,
extraordinarily like the goodness, say, of God,
something scented *and weeping in the evening dew.*

The zoo closes,
the horned owl dozes,
his dinner is done
and the bunnies are dead,
the green runs red,

see how they run
underneath the water where the sharks do fly
my, oh my!
underneath the water where the sharks do fly.

III   AN UPPER ROOM

Where is the world? Upstairs.
At the end of the corridor. The last room.
I have drawn the curtains back, under the window
I am waiting for my students, my sixty-first
year is high cloud that alters as it filters
the sun, good light while it lasts, for reading.
I can hear them growing up the stairs.

Goosey goosey gander
Whither do you wander?

Our book is open. Volcanic islets visit
over the top of the tide which is full, and full
of dead men's images, pouring into the room
Through the dear might of Him that walk'd the waves.
(Could you do that? Keep clear of the margins.
Here my line starts and it finishes *here,*
no later than the light lasts.)

We speak only
to each other but as if a third were present,
the thing we say.

Smaller than thought can think
the hours between us shrink,
books wink, volcanic islets sink
below that brink,
black margin, blind white ink.

There I found an old man
Who wouldn't say his prayers.

Dead bunnies. Blinded teddy bears.

IV AGENDA

A man who has never visited the Uffizi
isn't educated. English remark.

Be a playboy at 35. South British Insurance.
Picture of man fishing, from boat, with bottle.

Enjoy sex and stop breeding. Message to the age
from the Doctors Kronhausen, on waking.

V DO IT YOURSELF

Make it what height you like, the
sky will not fall nor will the dead
president rise because of his

> O
> B
> E
> L
> I
> S
> K
> 5
> 5
> 5
> f
> t
> .

nor is it any wonder that it is
one measured mile down river to the

> P   I
> A   T
> C   O   L

one measured mile up river to the

> L I N C
> M   O
> E   L
> M   N

O R I A L I
N C O L N M E
M O R I A L I N
With a few simple tools the handyman
can erect his thought upon Waiheke, volcanic islet,
lat. 37S long. 175E for the time being.

Read the instructions carefully.

VI NAMES ARE NEWS

A wood god botherer stands
not fifty feet from his own
door, calls trees by name.

Speak up we can't hear you.

Metrosideros robusta,
the northern rata. Usually
commencing life as an epiphyte
becomes a tall, massive tree
60 to 100 feet high.

Louder please.

Flowers are broad, dense,
terminal, many-flowered cymes,
dark scarlet.

What?

Dark scarlet.
Don't lean that weight! I call.
Shall I make you feel the full
rigour of a description?

Close!

For godsake no.

Closer.

Lord, I am small.
I break easily. I call
red cumulus green bubbled
cloud with a bloody curd,
not flowers, not cymes.
How fast do I have to talk?

Talk.

Seed vessels fly
forty thousand feet high
jetting towards a dark
destination up, up!
Funny how the sexual jets
grumbling aloft resemble
cymes, dark scarlet.
Can a machine do more?
Tall, massive clouds,
thunderheaded trees,
don't commence life that way.
Green pod, sky boring jet
nevertheless resemble.

Birds whistle and shit.

Lord,
I cannot compel you,
I implore you, by the dust
of a rigorous description
cracked by its own rigour,
lean easier, for the sake
of a chance resemblance.

Dark stays. Light goes.

Dark scarlet, inhuman,
silent in the fly-simmering
January sunlight
suffers no disguise,
description, resemblance.

A wood god botherer darkens
a moment his own doorstep,
enters, writes quickly,
adds a postscript.

The *New Zealand Herald* comes
late here, with the milk.
That was last week, the
pathologist's evidence
described the dead brother's
body, the burned-out farmstead,
what fat was burned away,
what skin, what battering the
skull *sustained* before the
Fire. And the oil-feed.
And the living brother by the rigour
of a description *stood*
erect, and the Court covered its
embarrassment, and ours, by the
rigour that was its only
rigour, of a description.

Flowers are broad, dense,
terminal

Louder please.

Jetting towards a dark
destination up, up!
It's a long long fall and a crack like doom
between the martinis and the satchels
up there and the dark down here.
Far too many flies, birds, worms, to begin with,
and that's not the end.

No.

Adam was no fool. He knew that at his age
a man must plan for his retirement. Or else.
He saw no better way than back to the bush.

An image in disrepair could study itself
in a pool, or such distraction from itself
as a bird flashing a scale upon his ear.

There was Cain to take over the business. There were
      signs.
Light no fires. Discharge no firearms.
Ten acre block for sale. Your private kingdom.

Lianes noosed harmlessly, the water ran
down above and below the road ran down
primevally babbling. Close to the foot

of a young totara, *Podocarpus hallii*,
Adam stumbled, and very nearly fell
over an old survey peg, half rotted.

If it blew like the wrath of God it was all blown over
ages ago, the angel hooked it, having lashed
round with a sword in a flaming bad temper.

Regeneration, conservation, were words
with which he comforted his mind, if angels,
vandals, vermin, got muddled in his mind.

Cain used to come over at the week-ends
and bring the children, who loved it.
Something must be done with it when the old man went.

VIII THE KITCHEN CUPBOARD

Sun, moon, and tides.
With the compliments of the *New Zealand Herald*
and Donaghy's Industries Limited makers
of the finest cordage since 1876.
Look on the inside of the cupboard door,
the middle one, on the left of the sink-bench.

All the bays are empty, a quick-drying wind
from the south-west browns the grey silt
the ebb-tide printed sexily, opulently,
making Nature's art nouveau, little as it matters
to mudlarking crabs and the morning's blue heron.

Olive, olive-budded, mangroves wait for the turn,
little as it means, to call that waiting.

A green car follows a blue car passing a brown car
on the Shore Road beyond the mangroves which wait
no more than the tide does because nothing waits.
Everything happens at once. It is enough.

That is not to say there is nothing to cry about,
only that the poetry of tears is a dead cuckoo.

The middle one, on the left of the sink-bench.
I stuck it on with sellotape. Not quite straight.

IX A DEAD LAMB

Never turn your back on the sea.
The mumble of the fall of time is continuous.

A billion billion broken waves deliver
a coloured glass globe at your feet, intact.

You say it is a Japanese fisherman's float.
It is a Japanese fisherman's float.

A king tide, a five o'clock low, is perfect
for picking mussels, picking at your ankle-bones.

The wind snaps at the yellow-scummed sea-froth,
so that an evanescence of irised bubbles occurs.

Simply, silverly the waves walk towards you.
A ship has changed position on the horizon.

The dog lifts a leg against a grass-clump
on a dune, for the count of three, wetting the sand.

There is standing room and much to be thankful for
in the present. Look, a dead lamb on the beach.

X   A FRAMED PHOTOGRAPH

The renaissance was six months old.
All the Kennedys were living at that time.
Jackie was hanging pictures in the White House.
I figured he could use the experience, Jack hornered,
when he starts in legal practice, naming Bobby
for Attorney-General.

Act one, scene one,
of the bloody melodrama. Everyone listened
while everyone read his poems. BANG! BANG!
and we cried all the way to My Lai.

To be silverly framed,
stood on the Bechstein, dusted daily
by the Jamaican girl whose eyes refuse them,
seeing alien Friendship one prolonged avenue
infinitely dusted, is a destiny which simply,
silverly they walk towards, towards my chair,
what jaunty pair
smiling the air
that flutters their trousers on Capitol Hill?
Why, Hiroshima Harry and the dandy Dean,

dust free. Heavenly muse!
fresh up your drink and sing.

What, exactly,
did he do at the Pentagon? He guessed he was
a deputy assistant secretary of defence,
a political appointment, modestly confided.
Hospitably home at cocktail time he took
one careful gin and tonic, excused himself
to mind State papers.

Dust the Bechstein, Anna.
Dust the megagothic national cathedral.
Dust destiny.

Fresh up. There is plenty of ice.

Receptacle, receive me.

XI   TWO PEDESTRIANS WITH ONE THOUGHT

Things are things carried
away by the wind like this
big empty carton which
bumps as it skids as it
arse-over-kites over
anything else that's loose
dust, for instance, while
    all the little angels
    ascend up ascend up
things are things emptied
on the tip of the wind
arsey-versey vortically
big print for instance
APPLE JUICE nothing in the
world ever catches its
carton again where the
wind went ƎƆIՈſ Ǝ˥dd∀
loose as the dust or the

water or the road or the
blood in your heels while
all the little angels
ascend up on high
all the little

God!
That was close, that bus
bloody nearly bowled the
both of them the dog with his
hindleg hiked and
APPLE JUICE bumped off the
wind's big boot
                    angels
          ascend up
hang on there
as long as you can
you and your dog before the
wind skins the water off the
road and the road off the
face of the earth
                    on high
          which end up?
          Arse end up
full beam by daylight
this funeral goes grinning, a
lively clip, a tail wind, the
grave waiting
hang on to your hands
anything can happen
once where the wind went
fingers you feel to be
nailed so securely
can come loose too
hold on to your ears and
run dog run while
simply, silverly
they walk in the wind that is
rippling their trousers
Hiroshima Harry and the
dandy Dean
dust free dusted while

> *all the little angels*
> *ascend up ascend up*
with
Plato in the middle
holding out his diddle in the
way souls piddle from a
very great height and
dead against the wind,
dead against the wind.

XII MAGNIFICAT

Who hasn't sighted Mary
        as he hung hot-paced
by the skin of the humped highway
        south from Waikanae
three hundred feet above the
        only life-sized ocean?
Tell me, mother of mysteries,
        how long is time?

Twelve electric bulbs
        halo Mary's head,
a glory made visible
        six feet in diameter,
two hundred and forty-five feet
        of solid hill beneath.
Tell me, mother of the empty grave,
        how high is heaven?

Mary's blessed face
        is six-and-a-half feet long,
her nose eighteen inches,
        her hands the same.
Conceived on such a scale,
        tell me, Dolorosa,
how sharp should a thorn be?
        how quick is death?

Mary's frame is timbered
  of two-by-four,
lapped with scrim and plastered
  three inches thick.
Westward of Kapiti
  the sun is overturned.
Tell me, Star of the Sea,
  what is darkness made of?

Mary has a manhole
  in the back of her head.
How else could a man get down there
  for maintenance, etc?
Mary is forty-seven feet,
  and that's not tall.
Tell me, by the Bread in your belly,
  how big is God?

I AM THE IMMACULATE
  CONCEPTION says
Mary's proud pedestal.
  Her lips concur.
Masterful giantess,
  don't misconceive me,
tell me, mother of the Way,
  where is the world?

XIII   A FOUR LETTER WORD

I

A wood god bothering cantor
rolls out his call. He names

tanekaha, kaiwaka, taraire.
Mispronounced, any of these

can strike dead and dumb. Well spoken,
they are a noise neither of the writhing root

nor glabrous leaf nor staring flower,
all that can unspeakably supervene.

II

Tane mahuta is a very big tree,
because of the signboards at the roadside.

Tired trunk, punky at the heart,
disyllabic Tane is too venerable

for words. True, that at a given sign
they stop their cars and walk no distance

to have seen, to have found themselves,
as advertised, in the absence of the god,

to have decently exposed some inches of film
in honour of his great girth.

Strike him with lightning!
the old arboreal bore.

Cut him up for signboards. Just look at that,
such longevity, such bulk, such lumbering tonnage.

III

Titans were titanic in the old days
before the defoliant Thunderer.

The children had no fathers then, as now.
No nativity ode for Tane. At his namegiving

nobody had the time, having time only
short of an unspeakable supervention

to blurt him, Logos begotten of log,
the disyllable, as he came.

In the technologies nothing can be done
without a divine sub-contract:

this one for the felling, the hollowing,
prone canoe, erected post;

Tane demiurgos,
lord of an obsolete skill:

not to keep an old man ticking
with a dead boy's heart

(cut while warm, after the crash,
pray for this tissue not to be rejected);

an instance now, look at it like that,
of what can unspeakably supervene,

ever since like cats in the dead of night
the first heaven and the first earth

coupled and begot,
and the theogonies littered the place

with the lordliest imaginable
stumps. That's life. That's fear

of this unspeakable that smashed the mouth
open, stamped on the balls and

ripped from the tongue's root, womb syllabled,
Tane, Tane mahuta.

XIV BOURDON

Spring thunder thumps on Friendship,
    high hands divide, collide,
let lightning down and wet the town,
    blinding the riverside
where Lincoln stares but never sees
what Washington is up to.
That cloud-cuffed shaft, those stony knees,
heaven's thunderstruck antipodes
    discover, arse-end up too.

The matrix cracks, the god still born
    stares his measured mile,
marble trousered, marble browed,
    throned in classical style.
Stone eyelids grind, a stony throat
    chokes with cherry bloom.
The matrix cracks again, again!
Sifting riverwards in the rain
a slow detritus dusts the brain
    under a sunless dome.

Thunder is a bluejay cock and a hen
    and a roll of the wrists,
the gods alone are solid stone
    dressed like beasts.
Rain courses down the stone, the stairs,
    and the knees that wear
stone still, a stony gaze is
snug as a bullet, smooth as phrases,
    the well plugged sepulchre.

They were doing their thing in the burning fiery furnace,
you couldn't hear the flute, harp, sackbut, psaltery
and all kinds of music for the silence of the flames.
Everything was very quiet in the heart of the furnace.

The wine was red, the acrylic was vermilion,
the pictures on the walls were hanging by their nails.
The needle was a diamond paddling in the bloodstream
issuing from the heart of the silence of the furnace,

streaming where it paddled in the stream that it was,
homing on the centre never to be punctured.
All the holy children were dancing on the needle
doing nothing but their thing in the burning fiery furnace,

Shadrach and Shakeback and Meshach and Sheshach
and Abednego and gay to bed we go along and upwards
of a hundred holy children in the burning fiery furnace.
It was dead still and silent at the centre of the disc.

There was the golden image, balls to the golden image,
balls to Nebuchadnezzar the king who set it up.
Not a note was audible over the silence of the flames,
of the psaltery and the dulcimer and all kinds of music.

Came the holy cold of morning, with all kinds of music
raking out the furnace, when their thing was done,
and which child broke silence, squeaking from the ashes,
issuing from the music of the flute, harp, etc.,

Shadrach or Shakeback or Meshach or Sheshach,
or gay to bed we go along with Abednego or whom?
growing up the stone stair, issuing from the music,
sucking on a diamond like an apricot stone, saying

There I found an old man who wouldn't say his prayers,
I took him by the sackbut and threw him down the stairs,
I adore Doctor Logos, but Yeats is so mysterious,
because he doesn't communicate *like Shakespeare does to me.*

XVI THERE IS A PLEASURE IN THE PATHLESS WOODS

When the green grenade explodes, does the kauri
experience an orgasm of the spent cone?
What is the king fern doing with its hairy knuckles?
Wildling and epiphyte, do they have problems too?
There's a reason for the spastic elbow of this taraire.
Look hard at nature. It is in the nature
of things to look, and look back, harder.
Botany is panic of another description.

XVII LONE KAURI ROAD

Too many splashes, too many gashes,
too big and too many holes in the west wall:
one by one the rectangles blazed and blacked where the
sun fell out of its frame, the time of the day
hung round at a loose end, lopsided.

It was getting desperate, even a fool could see,
it was feverish work, impossible to plug them all.
Even a fool, seeing the first mountain fall
out not into the sea or the smoking west but into
the places where these had been, could see the spider
brushed up, dusted, shovelled into the stove, and
how fast his legs moved, without the least surprise.

A tui clucked, shat, whistled thrice.
My gaze was directed where the branch had been.
An engine fell mute into the shadow of the valley
where the shadow had been.

XVIII   ANY TIME NOW

Extraordinary things happen every day
in our street only this morning
the ground opened at my feet
without warning
unless it was a cloud in the south
balled like a swelling in the mouth.

And the air was fresh, being winter
time when the ground broke
disclosing a billion bodies burning
under a thin smoke.
Was it then that I saw in my walk   `
an eggshell, a capsicum stalk?

Such details are always so terribly
(if that is the word) distinct
as grit under the eyelid, like today
when the ground blinked,
disclosing what never should be seen.
Walking is a pleasure, I mean.

Fortunately there was not very much
traffic and no kiddies playing,
couldn't have picked a better day for it
I was just saying
when the ground closed over the sky
hollow as the cloud was high.

from

A Small Room with Large Windows

(1962)

A SMALL ROOM WITH LARGE WINDOWS

i

What it would look like if really there were only
One point of the compass not known illusory,
All other quarters proving nothing but quaint
Obsolete expressions of true north (would it be?),
And seeds, birds, children, loves and thoughts bore down
The unwinding abiding beam from birth
To death! What a plan!
                                    Or parabola.
You describe yours, I mine, simple as that,
With a pop and a puff of nonchalant stars up top,
Then down, dutiful dead stick, down
(True north all the way nevertheless).

One way to save space and a world of trouble.

A word on arrival, a word on departure.
A passage of proud verse, rightly construed.
An unerring pen to edit the ensuing silences
(That's more like it).

ii

                        Seven ageing pine trees hide
Their heads in air but, planted on bare knees,
Supplicate wind and tide. See if you can
See it (if this is it), half earth, half heaven,
Half land, half water, what you call a view
Strung out between the windows and the tree trunks;
Below sills a world moist with new making where
The mangrove race number their cheated floods.
Now in a field azure rapidly folding
Swells a cloud sable, a bad bitching squall
Thrashes the old pines, has them twitching
Root and branch, rumouring a Götterdämmerung.
Foreknowledge infects them to the heart.
                                    Comfortable

To creak in tune, comfortable to damn
Slime-suckled mangrove for its muddy truckling
With time and tide, knotted to the vein it leeches.

iii

In the interim, how the children should be educated,
Pending a decision, a question much debated
In our island realms. It being, as it is,
Out of the question merely to recognize
The whole three hundred and sixty degrees,
Which prudence if not propriety forbids,
It is necessary to avail oneself of aids
Like the Bible, or no Bible, free swimming tuition,
Art, sex, no sex and so on. Not to direct
So much as to normalize personality, protect
From all hazards of climate, parentage, diet,
Whatever it is exists. While, on the quiet,
It is understood there is a judgement preparing
Which finds the compass totally without bearing
And the present course correct beyond a doubt,
There being two points precisely, one in, one out.

iv

A kingfisher's naked arc alight
Upon a dead stick in the mud
A scarlet geranium wild on a wet bank
A man stepping it out in the near distance
With a dog and a bag
                              on a spit of shell
On a wire in a mist
                              a gannet impacting
Explode a dozen diverse dullnesses
Like a burst of accurate fire.

AN OPPRESSIVE CLIMATE, A POPULOUS NEIGHBOURHOOD

I

I look from this back window straight across
To that back window and there see standing
In the through-current rippling his white vest and briefs
A grey-headed man who turns, retreats, returns
(For the coolness, no doubt, of linoleum to the naked sole)

And looks from that back window straight across
To this back window and there sees standing
In the through-current naked but for my white briefs
A brown-headed man. Put it that we note and respect
Each other's individuality, he is not chagrined

Because I am content with briefs and reject the vest,
Nor is my own free spirit offended because he
Cannot comfortably acquiesce. This inspection complete,
I too turn from the rear and pad the apartment through
(For the coolness, truly, of linoleum to the naked sole)

To the street-front window and there see a brown-thighed girl
Crotched on a ground-floor sill. One up and to the right
A blue nightgown bodilessly gets out of bed
And passes from view. A boy rearranges his pillow.
I pan to the flight above, a hand shifts a pot-plant

From the sill, one hand, the perfection of anonymity.
What we cherish is our own business, this hand innocently
Withdraws its treasure. Put it simply that the owner may be stripped
Naked for the heat and has nothing to hide but himself.
Satisfied, I put no impertinent question to myself

Concerning these companions, least of all any literary question.
Hell, let's face it, is horribly hot and overcrowded,
But where else do you find the niceties of neighbourly regard
More observed and the mitigable nuisance of neighbourly love
Better understood than in this City we have been building so long?

A dog howls all morning Saturday.
His inhuman frequencies
Touch like sad art with its astonishing
Human unlikenesses.

Somebody tied the poor dog up
In the hinder-precinct of some brownstone,
And shut the door and the garden gate
And went out, and left him alone.

Thickly in this thick heat the dog
Ululates, convoking the neighbours, sày,
500 to 600 East 84th and 85th streets,
To tell of some too far away

Catastrophe, some canine Cathay
Scourged by earthquake or famine –
Some disaster in Canis Major our myopic
Instruments cannot examine.

Dog, dog, I'm tied up too.
Be my guest, my metaphor.
Be Fool to my Lear till the neighbours hear
And maybe open the door.

The dog howls. It's a dog howling.
If it warbled, it would be a bird.
If we don't make ourselves intelligible,
We make ourselves heard.

Dog, dog, they will come and untie you.
You shall have a pat and a bone,
And a run with the Gracie Square dogs
To whom you are personally known.

My telephone doesn't ring of itself –
That calls for the human hand.
Dog, dog, all it takes is patience,
Which dogs don't understand.

New York, July 1961

from
Poems 1949 – 1957
(1957)

A LEAF

The puzzle presented by any kind of a leaf,
One among millions to smudge your airy sceneries
Or among millions one your window tickler
Gust upon gust agitates, a trifle sharp
Enough to murder sleep:

Shape of a leaf, shine of a leaf,
Shade of a leaf yellow among yellow leaves of
The prophet Micah with a slip of perished silk
Marks nothing, still is a character, a syllable
Made flesh before the word:

Bud of a leaf, blade of a leaf
Given a strange twist, given for something to do
With deadly baffled fingers happy to squeeze
Blood from a conundrum: insoluble but endlessly
Amusing in the attempt.

TO FORGET SELF AND ALL

To forget self and all, forget foremost
This whimpering second unlicked self my country,
To go like nobody's fool an ungulled ghost
By adorned midnight and the pitch of noon
Commanding at large everywhere his entry,
Unimaginable waterchinks, granular dark of a stone?
Why that'd be freedom heyday, hey
For freedom that'd be the day
And as good a dream as any to be damned for.

Then to patch it up with self and all and all
This tousled sunny-mouthed sandy-legged coast,
These painted and these rusted streets,
This heart so supple and small,
Blinding mountain, deafening river
And smooth anxious sheets,

And go like a sober lover like nobody's ghost?
Why that'd be freedom heyday, hey
Freedom! That'd be the day
And as good a dream as any to be damned to.

To sink both self and all why sink the whole
Phenomenal enterprise, colours shapes and sizes
Low like Lucifer's bolt from the cockshied roost
Of groundless paradise: peeled gold gull
Whom the cracked verb of his thoughts
Blew down blew up mid-air, where the sea's gorge rises,
The burning brain's nine feathering fathom doused
And prints with bubbles one grand row of noughts?
Why that'd be freedom heyday, hey
For freedom, that'd be the day
And as good a dream as any to be damned by.

THE EYE IS MORE OR LESS SATISFIED WITH SEEING

Wholehearted he can't move
   From where he is, nor love

Wholehearted that place,
   Indigene janus-face,

Half mocking half,
   Neither caring to laugh.

Does true or false sun rise?
   Do both half eyes tell lies?

Cradle or grave, which view's
   The actual of the two?

Half eyes foretell, forget
   Sunrise, sunset,

Or closed a fraction's while
   Half eyes half smile

Upon light the spider lid
  Snares, holds hid

And holds him whole (between
  The split scarves of that scene)

Brimming astride a pulse
  Of moon-described eyeball's

Immobile plenitude –
  Flower of the slight stemmed flood.

Snap open! He's all eyes, wary,
  Darting both ways one query,

Whether the moonbeam glanced
  Upon half to whole enhanced,

Or wholly the soul's error
  And confederate mirror.

IDYLLS IN COLOUR FILM

i. *Cristobal*

Top to bottom of a skin white wall
Some thin vine blossom bleeds, the sun
Indolently erodes the sill.
Blood can run cold in this hot town.

And the blue sky bends a very smooth look
And the water keeps malignant calm
And the itchy mouth the Canal has makes
Lips to compress their ocean's arm.

Fat with colour the day commands
Holstered, blazing boss of the street.
Time daren't stir, nor the four winds.
Death is detained, but won't be late.

Cool off at El Tropico; fans,
Cans, fans and a glassful which
Can't go bad like the barrow man's
Bag of oranges while you watch.

Polyglot, polychrome droop or blow
Lush hybrids of the dollar shallows.
Nylon blooms and rags in a row,
Negress purples, negress yellows

Shame without strutting step or breast
Pale casual trash two hours ashore;
From bodily darkness have digressed
By a flowery shift of skins, no more.

Now continents and oceans lie
Farther than planets, and the scarlet
Or bruise-blue petals kiss your knee,
Romancing in an isthmian twilight

Of temperate islands.
                              The Zone Troops
Strike MacArthurian attitudes.
Avid the traveller slums the shops,
Tickling a vein which no blood leads

That street where one was knifed last night.
Home and aboard is where to be,
With a mast-high moon, eyes crackling bright.
The Caribbean's the next sea.

ii. *Curacao*

The slimed embrasures of old fortress walls
Green lower-lipped outside Saint Anna Bay
Cannot articulate: this hoarse wind smells
Of oil; two hundred tankers night and day

Hod El Dorado past the Bridge of Boats
Up the foul stream and down. The Dutch façades
Cold and small as coral are the sights
Most photographed: but memory knows no aids

One mile from Willemstad (past midnight, that
Refiner's fire across the basin mimes
Hell but fools nobody) while we set foot
Again on the low desolate slope whose name's

Nothing and nowhere: fingering the leaf-shuttered
Inconsequence of streets. For the wind here's
Close and vigilant, misses no flitted
Grain or leaf, watches each step, cares

For every stone in Hoogstraat.
                         Have we lived
Anywhere if not here, walking alone
Through dreams or deaths awake, having arrived
One hour ago, by morning to be gone?

ELEGY ON MY FATHER

Tremayne Curnow, of Canterbury, New Zealand, 1880-1949

Spring in his death abounds among the lily islands,
There to bathe him for the grave antipodean snows
Fall floodlong, rivermouths all in bloom, and those
Fragile church timbers quiver
By the bourne of his burial where robed he goes
No journey at all. One sheet's enough to cover
My end of the world and his, and the same silence.

While in Paddington autumn is air-borne, earth-given,
Day's nimbus nearer staring, colder smoulders;
Breath of a death not my own bewilders
Dead calm with breathless choirs
O bird-creation singing where the world moulders!
God's poor, the crutched and stunted spires
Thumb heavenward humorously under the unriven

Marble November has nailed across their sky:
Up there, dank ceiling is the dazzling floor
All souls inhabit, the lilied seas, no shore
My tear-smudged map mislimned.
When did a wind of the extreme South before
Mix autumn, spring and death? False maps are dimmed,
Lovingly they mock each other, image and eye.

The ends of the earth are folded in his grave
In sound of the Pacific and the hills he tramped singing,
God knows romantically or by what love bringing
Wine from a clay creek-bed,
Good bread; or by what glance the inane skies ringing
Lucidly round; or by what shuffle or tread
Warning the dirt of miracles. Still that nave

He knelt in puts off its poor planks, looms loftier
Lonelier than Losinga's that spells in stone
The Undivided Name. *Oh quickening bone*
Of the Mass-priest under grass
Green in my absent spring, sweet relic atone
To our earth's Lord for the pride of all our voyages,
That the salt winds which scattered us blow softer.

London, November 1949

EVIDENCES OF RECENT FLOOD

> *Adam and Eve and Pinch Me*
> *Went down to the river to bathe,*
> *Adam and Eve were drowned,*
> *And who do you think was saved?*

I
Logbook Found on Ararat

Only one night the
                    squall made a great show,
thunderclaps fit to burst,
                    mightily flapped

linens and lightnings,
            heaven's menagerie leapt
loose upon decks
           and the herd snarled below.

Calm yawned by dawn
           assuaged our seafaring
staring by some land's lamp
           outlimbed, so gloomy,
less than it loomed a
           withering gulf could show me,
but snuffed-out beacons
           uncaring, uncuring:

blindalleyed seaways,
           suburban promontories.
Dogging a dumb spark,
           diamond in the spine
(dead by my reckoning
           both the red and the green),
my only ship shaped home
           lonelier than seas

pattering at the prow
           between pouring deeps:
fearfully at flood-peak
           unfathomed my ark
the dove-watch kept
           in cages of wickerwork,
bickering and bloody
           the beaks and claw-tips:

no not fair-feathered
           upon the first isles
these cage-birds thwarted
           at each other's throats;
though landward upon a lipping
           liquor she floats
and flood no more now
           than upon sands prevails.

Groping for moorings
                    the grave side of dawn
God! horrorstruck we see
                    from what hoodwinking hidden
wrecks gasped the rescued
                    grew some certainty
love soiled some shore yet
                    Oh some sheer crown

of the earth rage overlooked
                    I look-out stared
at mirrorstricken my own
                    land manfully back:
all I steered mists to gain by
                    drowning, luck
or the All-Duplicity on
                    high had spared:

the cocks crescent
                    upon crags and sills
the seed surgent in
                    brine-sodden furrows
the girl congealed in smiling
                    salt, all sorrows
shambling, All-Shallows
                    in a slough of souls.

None here could drown
                    though thou God jerk the bells
unfathomable steeplejacked
                    rungs below:
mockers when thy rains wreathed,
                    ripe mockers now,
the obsolete polyp
                    sobbing in their skulls:

and their lame talk pursues
                    prediluvian lines
and all weather or never
                    is thy Name's news spoken
and those mortal talons
                    of the dove not mistaken

and thy deluge a dribble
                    whose drunken ebb sucks
bald an earth born to us
                    of shipwreck, hooked
by the gills on Ararat,
                    grounded for our pains.

II

A Changeling

Once where the leaky
                    islands and the lame
swimmers ducked
                    and draked between earshots
of stars and oceans
                    there plummeted a fulgent
freak with unwebbed
                    fingers, a girl kind of
fish whose fire and
                    water works and bellied
moon waxing in the summer
                            seascape bared
(with her light like ashes
                    of a god absconded)
our home hill-toppled town
                            grown cold as wishes.

Lithe she unlocked
                    the circuit of the harbour
tickled she fore and aft
                            the daft old sulking
bottoms, with her tail tipped
                            many a green
mooring-chain, diving in a
                            weedy boy's skull
her small bell sang.
                    Such miracles of the lovers
and fishes followed her
                    that sodden straw

sparked, sat up and glared like some
                              god-bonfired navy
most classically scuttled, glory's
                              dredges dismasted.

Swim! spied our laddery
                    town from all its rungs;
corks, bladders and the last
                    breath beat the surges;
till her sunken silver
                    filleted in the main
of mankind wilted
                    on the bright tide's verge.
Hooked and played
                    and laid upon the sands
loose she lay
                    under the yellow lupin.
Cold fell the quiet coast,
                    midnight looming
and the midnight ebb
                    and when it struck she rose

up lightly, her stains
                    were silken, she shook out
her hair in the teeth of the
                    tide's thunder so
idly that the moon
                    sank without a cry
nor dared we more than dumbly
                    trail her tiny
mortal steps deep down
                    to the town train.
Listen! those whistles
                    down our line to the grave.
Listen! those bells
                    to toll the changeling home
ding at the ebb, ocean,
                    dong at the flood.

Sob, shabby islands
                    in your dull weeds doting
on a fleeting fable
                    a feather in the sun.
All your white horse
                    wishes would not wash
one white shell from the
                    wave the changeling swam.
She's home and dry
                    and high among the ladders
as plain as daylight that's
                    back like an old debt,
drowned swimmers in her eyes
                    and stars, and oceans,
her comb and her glass
                    and her ticket in her hand.

WHEN THE HULK OF THE WORLD

When the hulk of the world whirls again between
Us for the ships shift me where your dusk is dawn
   My skyblue side of the globe,
Where the mooncast squid's eye of a downcast ocean
Goggles till it gets me in the beam of its brine –
   Oh then, sweet claustrophobe
I leave among the lost leaves of a London wood
(So dark, we missed the middle of our road)
   Can spring condone, redeem
One treachery of departure from that life,
Shiftless to fetch this love?
   Seas will be seas, the same;
Thick as our blood may flood, our opposite isles
Chase each other round till the quiet poles
   Crack, and the six days top
Totter, but catch us neither sight nor hold;
Place will be place, limbs may not fold
   Their natural death in dreams.
I pray, pray for me on some spring-wet pavement

Where halts the heartprint of our salt bereavement,
    Pray over many times,
Forgive him the seas forgive him the spring leaf,
All bloom ungathered perishable as grief,
    For the hulk of the world's between
And I go as a ghost, one flesh I and the wind
That lifts us both so lightly, but so bound
    Never to be ghost alone.

SPECTACULAR BLOSSOM

Mock up again, summer, the sooty altars
Between the sweltering tides and the tin gardens,
All the colours of the stained bow windows.
Quick, she'll be dead on time, the single
Actress shuffling red petals to this music,
Percussive light! So many suns she harbours
And keeps them jigging, her puppet suns,
All over the dead hot calm impure
Blood noon tide of the breathless bay.

Are the victims always so beautiful?

Pearls pluck at her, she has tossed her girls
Breast-flowers for keepsakes now she is going
For ever and astray. I see her feet
Slip into the perfect fit the shallows make her
Purposefully, sure as she is the sea
Levels its lucent ruins underfoot
That were sharp dead white shells, that will be sands,
The shallows kiss like knives.

Always for this
They are chosen for their beauty.

Wristiest slaughterman December smooths
The temple bones and parts the grey-blown brows
With humid fingers. It is an ageless wind
That loves with knives, it knows our need, it flows

Justly, simply as water greets the blood,
And woody tumours burst in scarlet spray.
An old man's blood spills bright as a girl's
On beaches where the knees of light crash down.
These dying ejaculate their bloom.

Can anyone choose
And call it beauty? – The victims
Are always beautiful.

IN MEMORY OF DYLAN THOMAS

And the Lord God formed man of the dust of the
ground, and breathed into his nostrils the breath of
life; and man became a living soul.

Never a talking but a telling breath
Fanned fire from clay upright to the tip of his tongue,
Who burning to tell told all the days of his death
It was the ghost alive in a beast's lung
Panting for-ever out.
Now the five gates are shut,
The grassy fingers sheathed in enough dust,
And the last work, at most, is what all must.

He hardly knew what struck him the first spark
Bursting the bolts of sense upon the frame
Of things. It was light outraging the pure dark.
It was the ghost buried alive in time,
Purse-lipped for pain,
That blew upon his brain
The iridescent sweaty swarms that rose
Winged imagos, out of their wormy throes.

Adam and Eve behind the village bethel
Played snakes and ladders. Bibles were hot to touch;
He laid his open on the cool of a sill, the wrath all
Feared he fondled; fruit-in-hand, found such
Were all men's bedfellows.
And he could never close

Genesis for appleblossom's joy, our tripping
First girl and boy in plucking time caught napping.

Self-scrutineer, with what pierced eyes he pored,
Live coals upon the body's private inches.
Shame in the ghost rebuffed what flesh adored,
But the game beast on a griddle heaved its haunches:
Sinful, infinitely worth
Saving, the beasts of earth
At the end of their tether either way, that fled
Between the matin-bell and midnight bed.

And he said, What hast thou done? the voice of thy
brother's blood crieth unto me from the ground.

A town boy, he trod
The earth beneath the pavements
And knew stones could bleed.
Storming bereavements
Inflamed his eyes. He was afraid

With the common fear that time
Of a blitzing sickness,
But under blood and blame
Exclaimed, so blazed his darkness
Genesis' thunderbolt shot home.

Irrational good, caged
In Faith's condemned cell, burning
Its own breast unassuaged –
Crybaby crying the morning
Stars out while Creation raged.

And out of the ground the Lord God formed every
beast of the field, and every fowl of the air; and
brought them unto Adam to see what he would call
them; and whatsoever Adam called every living
creature, that was the name thereof.

Laugharne village peters out an inch from the fishy bay
Whose rackless tides lightly incuriously rap their twice-a-day
Reminders to hewn human stone deaf as cockle shells

That a lifeless landscape suckles, fills and flushes the salt wells,
And the moon is a spirit.
                              By day by dead pearl calm
He valued the mere view of it the bare sea-moulded arm
Relaxed about slack water. Southward the ship shape
Of the shade of an isle is Lundy. Some lounging cape
Condescends to the vanishing west; a few miles that way brings
You, map-witted, to Pendine Sands.
                                    Mere living things
Crackle their moments out over the breath-heavy green
Foreshorelands, glimmers of Godhead not unseen
But often to crawl, creep, scamper, flit or fly,
Starting under his feet in the track of his eye
Who named them, with praise again as Adam unfallen had,
Praise that never to Adam fallen the Maker forbade.
Named the heron son of Zebedee fishing his moody shoal.
Named the congregation of crabs, dabs, waterbirds, the owl
So fell to fur, the ranger fox outsnapping a winter's cold.
Named, who never could have told
The tally of his heart's household.

A window shalt thou make to the ark, and in a cubit
shalt thou finish it above: and the door of the ark
shalt thou set in the side thereof; with lower, second,
and third storeys shalt thou make it.

    A stack of whitewashed stone
    Cramped square upon a lap of rock
    And butted endwise to a bushy bluff,
    One chink of the foreshore there,

    The house – locally known
    As Boathouse – house enough
    Or Ark at flood-time fit to bear
    Pigeon-postman Noah and all his stock.

And the Lord smelled a sweet savour: and the Lord
said in his heart, I will not again curse the ground
any more for man's sake; for the imagination of
man's heart is evil from his youth: neither will I
again smite any more every thing living, as I have
done.

Sir John's Hill. Bramble and scrubby growth
Humped not much higher than chimney-puff.
By tide-scurf, dead weed, up and over the path
Ramble, far-fetching scholar, the brief rough

Prose of a broken landscape, summoning how
On this earth, out of all rare wringers
Of hands and hearts one here saw heaven's bent brow
Pitifully judging birds and singers.

'Ware the hawk, 'ware the hill,
Claw clenched for the trilling throat,
The shadow, the shudder, the kill,
Feathers afloat –

But in the map of mercy among a city's
Dying millions he fell,
Who chose of heaven's thousand thousand pities
The sparrow's one, and all.

KEEP IN A COOL PLACE

A bee in a bloom on the long hand of a floral
Clock can't possibly tell the right time
And if it could whatever would the poor bee do with it
In insufferably hot weather like this?

Everything white looks washed, at the correct distance
And may be the correct distance. You could eat
Our biggest ship sweet as sugar and space can make her.
Every body's just unwrapped, one scrap of a shaving

Left for luck or the look, the maker's seal intact,
Glad to be genuine! The glassy seaside's
Exact to the last detail, tick of a tide,
Fluke of the wind, slant of a sail. The swimmers

On lawns and the athletes in cosy white beds have visitors
And more flowers. Poor bee! He can make up time
At frantic no speed, whether tick or tock,
Hour or minute hand's immaterial. That's

Exactly how it is now. It is. It is
Summer all over the striped humming-top of the morning
And what lovely balloons, prayer-filled (going up!) to fluke
For once and for all the right time, the correct distance.

TO INTRODUCE THE LANDSCAPE

To introduce the landscape to the language
Here on the spot, say that it can't be done
By kindness or mirrors or by talking slang
With a coast accent. Sputter your pieces one

By one like wet matches you scrape and drop:
No self-staled poet can hold a candle to
The light he stares by. Life is the wrong shop
For pictures, you say, having all points and no view.

Ponderous pine wagging his wind-sopped brushes
Daubs Latin skies upon Chinese lagoons.
What tides leak through the mangroves and the rushes
Or lofted, wash long needles and large cones?

And where, from here, do you go? Out with the tide
You won't, without some word that will have lied.

DUNEDIN

for James K. Baxter

Is it window or mirror the enormous
Deforming glass propped on horizons here?
What did we see? Some town pinched in a pass
Across which stares perpetual startled sheer
Vacuous day, the kind blind wilderness,
Space put behind bars, face pushed too near:

Painfully upright among lost hills
Bowed under cloud, made fast to the shocked ships
Locked in an eddy, dwelling. There, none wills
Redress or dreams it, or pondering some lapse
Out of a dream strays back into that town
A mirage of the cracked antarctic stole,
Or stumbles on the original dazed stone
Pitched out of Scotland to the opposite Pole.

JACK-IN-THE-BOAT

> *is always ready to row across the bath or lake. Wind up the
> motor, and watch him dip his blades like a true oarsman –
> in, out, in, out – with never-tiring enthusiasm.*
>
> — LEGEND ON A TOY-MAKER'S PACKAGE

Children, children, come and look
Through the crack in the corner of the middle of the world
At the clockwork man in a cardboard house.
He's crying, children, crying.
  He's not true, really.

Once he was new like you, you see
Through the crack in the corner of the middle of the night,
The bright blue man on the wind-up sea,
Oh, he went so beautifully.
  He's not true, really.

O cruel was the pleasure-land they never should have painted
On the front and the back, the funny brand of weather,
For the crack in the corner of the middle of the picture
Let the colours leak away.
   He's not true, really.

One at a time, children, come and look
Through the crack in the corner of the middle of the day
At Jack-in-the-Boat where the light leaves float.
He's dying of a broken spring.
   He's not true, really.

MEMENTOS OF AN OCCASION

Wallace Stevens, 1879-1955

i

Dead but to the world, Stevens, do you find
The anecdotes lucid there, compared with these?

And what comparisons with your style when crossing
Composedly the blue thresholds to sit down
Oceans away (because all airs bore alike
And Indian-wise an alien offshore fragrance) –
Or mulch with moist real hands the seedy words
To bear in season as fresh-cut coxcomb blooms
As anyone else's green and god-sown country
Whose natives, planting and watering botany books,
Had their disappointments?

                        Can they be less alien
Or more at home, the breath-stopped kiss-shaped nomenclatures
Down where the dead are?

                        If we have all met somewhere
Elsewhere before?

ii

A well-set-up shade passed
Forth between ranting sun and rabble retina,
Announcing a prim masque, a conducted illusion
Out of worse nothing.

It was not quite as if
The snake, uniquely accomplished could slip in and
Out of the time-worn pelt experience till
Crackle! and lastly dry scurf popping
Nipped up thin air, dumbfounded all as-ifs –

iii

Let that have been as it may, you are the type
Should manage a vaporous shift of habitat
To where, if any can raise a squeak yours may be
Intelligible, as ghostliest counsel goes,
As poems, the ponderable these, are eligible,

iv

Capable to detect where reality was not
And scrupulous what to put in place of it.

HE CRACKED A WORD

He cracked a word to get at the inside
Of the inside, then the whole paper bag full
The man said were ripe and good.
The shrunken kernels
Like black tongues in dead mouths derided
The sillinesses of song and wagging wisdom:
These made a small dumb pile, the hopping shells
Froze to the floor, and those made patterns
Half-witted cameras glared at, finding as usual
Huge meteorites in mouseland.
What barefaced robbery!
He sat, sat, sat mechanically adding
To the small dumb pile, to the patterns on the floor,
Conscious of nothing but memories, wishes
And a faint but unmistakable pricking of the thumbs,
The beginnings of his joy.

from
At Dead Low Water
(1949)

CHILDREN, SWIMMERS

Children, swimmers, the whole brilliant harbour
Coveting the young bodies, how far drowned
Under the wrack-curdled tide of my mind
You are, and you fellow-swimmer deeper

Than all since I, envying every bead of the sea
Jewelling your skin, its passionate regard shining,
Coveted barely with a look, complaining
With a gooseflesh my numb thought in the warm day:

And saw the days pass, and upon the shrunken
Soot-sprinkled pool-green harbour the days pass:
Oh but how under sea glitters no less
Your flesh against time's fathoms, and not sunken

Ever, astonishes with a breath this drowned
Valley where tides are lost and love's dead found.

TOMB OF AN ANCESTOR

I. *In Memoriam, R.L.M.G.*

The oldest of us burst into tears and cried
Let me go home, but she stayed, watching
At her staircase window ship after ship ride
Like birds her grieving sunsets; there sat stitching

Grandchildren's things. She died by the same sea.
High over it she led us in the steepening heat
To the yellow grave; her clay
Chose that way home: dismissed, our feet

Were seen to have stopped and turned again down hill;
The street fell like an ink-blue river
In the heat to the bay, the basking ships, this Isle
Of her oblivion, our broad day. Heaped over

So lightly, she stretched like time behind us, or
Graven in cloud, our farthest ancestor.

II. *To Fanny Rose May*

Great-aunt, surviving of that generation
Whose blood sweetens the embittered seas between
Fabulous old England and these innovations
My mountainous islands: in the bright sad scene

I praise with you your voyage, and hers who sleeps
A sister folded in the hill cemetery,
Sacrifice or seed lodged on those slopes
That seem barbaric, by the unworshipped sea

Toward which she would shade her eyes. I know the fires
That forged the harbour and the heights glow still,
A million years old memory, but there's
Neither memory nor world here but that hill

Where struck your voyaging sister seed, from whom
I grow, and this praise flows, this blood, this name.

AT DEAD LOW WATER

I

At dead low water, smell of harbour bottom,
Sump of opulent tides; in foul chinks twirl
Weed and whorl of silt recoiling, clouding
The wan harbour sighing on all its beaches.

The boat was not deliberately abandoned
But tied here and forgotten, left afloat
Freakishly, bobbing where the summers foundered,
Jarring each wave the jetty's tettered limbs;

Worm carves wave polishes original shapes,
Bolt and knot give way, gaps in the decking
Turn up again, driftwood on other sands.
All drifts till fire or burial.

Life, trapped, remembers in the rancid shallows
What crept before the enormous strides of love
When the word alone was, and the waters:
Goes back to the beginning, the whole terror

Of time and patience. Bolt and strake are frilled
With the shrimp's forest, all green-bearded timbers.
Salt rocky chink, nude silted cleft give off
Birth smell, death smell. Mute ages tread the womb.

II

Nervous quiet not calm possesses
Sea water here, the wave turns wary
Finding itself so far inland.

The father with the child came down
First thing one morning, before any
Dreamt of visiting the beach; it was

Daylight but grey, midsummer; they
Crossed high-water mark, dry-shod,
Derelict shells, weed crisped or rotting,

Down to the spongy rim, slowly
Without fear, stepping hand in hand
Within an inch of the harmless sea

Pure, unfractured, many miles,
Still steel water sheathed between
Once violent hills, volcanic shapes.

O memory, child, what entered at the
Eye, ecstasy, air or water?
What at the mouth? But carefully

Morning by morning incorruption
Puts on corruption; nervously
Wave creeps in and lingers over

Tideswept heaps where the fly breeds:
Memory flows where all is tainted,
Death with life and life with death.

Twenty years. A child returned
Discerns in quicksand his own footprint
Brimming and fading, vanishing.

III

Failed at the one flood we do not count
On miracles again, and you may say
We die from now; while each amazed migrant
Waves back, and cannot tear his eyes away

From his own image, the weeping threatening
Accusing thing, and knows death does not rid
Him even of the deformed sunk sifted thing,
Memory's residue; because the dead,

Father and child, still walk the water's edge:
A kindness, an inconsequent pastime, froze
In time's tormented rock, became an age
When tropics shifted, buried rivers rose,

Meaningless but for individual pain
No death, no birth relieves or lunar pulses drown.

Governor's Bay, December 1944

OLD HAND OF THE SEA

Old hand of the sea feeling
Blind in sunlight for the salt-veined beaches
O setting on a tide my bearded boat a-sailing
Easy as the bird's breast that barely touches

Immemorial deeps of death:
Here, now, my harbour, child's play pool,
Sifter of sunk bright treasure, breaker of earth,
Is monster and lover of the gazing soul.

Horizons bloomed here on the globes of eyes,
Here grieving fog fastened those lids with tears
Disfiguring, transfiguring; holidays
Nested like bird or girl. All disappears

But the salt searching hand. O sightless tides
What blossom blows to you from spring hillsides?

EDEN GATE

The paper boat sank to the bottom of the garden
The train steamed in at the white wicked gate,
The old wind wished in the hedge, the sodden
Sack loved the yellow shoot;

And scampering children woke the world
Singing Happy Doomsday over all the green willows
That sprang like panic from the crotch of the cold
Sappy earth, and away in the withered hollows

A hand no warmer than a cloud rummaged
At the river's roots: up there in the sky
God's one blue eye looked down on the damaged
Boy tied by the string of a toy

And saw him off at the gate and the train
All over again.

WITH HOW MAD STEPS

Nightwatchman in some crater of the moon –
No, not that lunatic
But the dumb satellite itself, my tune
The cold sphere's silence; and I stick

(Abiding, law-abiding) to that orbit
Fire once described, tossed into space to cool
From my earth's body; a gyrating habit.
What if she watches? She'll

Mask with the mirror of her tides those shores
Her flesh makes in the heavens, and even`
While dawn destroys me her young foliage stirs;
Neither is mathematical space forgiven

My dear earth's distance, though her heart descry
With how mad steps, her moon, I climb the sky.

THE WAKING BIRD REFUTES

Rain's unassuaging fountains multiply
In air on earth and leaf. The Flood began
This way, listened to at windows by
The sleepless: one wept, one revolved a plan,

One died and rose again, one felt
That colder breath blow from the poles of lips
At love's meridian. This way now the spoilt
Firmament of the blood dissolves and drops;

The bright waste repossessive element
Beats barely audible, one sound imposing
Silence upon silence. This way I went
To pull our histories down, down, heavens accusing

Of rainbowed guile, whose penal rains descend.
The waking bird refutes: world will not end.

Milton made Eve his blonde, but she is dark
And dark is Eden where her tree ascends;
And yet she shines; no shy deer in God's park,
She's formidable. The fruit between her hands

Is moon to her deliberate earth; the cold
Smooth yellow rind of moon or fruit invites
Tongue, or on branch alight allures handhold.
Temptress, to darken her delights

Offers her apple with one withering leaf,
Ripeness and death in hand; imparts that knowledge,
Yet lovingly lets in the thief
Of innocence: moon-sodden foliage

Parted, lays her big limbs unshadowed bare
To the white clamberer's prehensile stare.

from
Sailing or Drowning
(1943)

DISCOVERY

How shall I compare the discovery of islands?
History had many instinctive processes
Past reason's range, green innocence of nerves,
Now all destroyed by self-analysis.

Or, out of God the separated streams
Down honeyed valleys, Minoan, Egyptian,
And latterly Polynesia like ocean rains,
Flowing, became one flood, one swift corruption;

Or, the mad bar-beating bird of the mind
Still finding the unknown intolerable
Burst into a vaster cage, contained by seas,
Prisoned by planets within the measurable;

Or, Gulliver with needles, guns, and glass,
Thrusting trinkets up from the amazing hatches,
Luring doll kings and popes off palm-tree perches,
Sold them the Age of Reason from the beaches;

Dazzle no more in the discoverer's eye
When his blind chart unglazes, foam and flower
Suddenly spilt on the retreating mirror,
Landfall undreamed or anchorage unsure.

Compare, compare, now horrible untruth
Rings true in our obliterating season:
Our islands lost again, all earth one island,
And all our travel circumnavigation.

OUT OF SLEEP

Awake, but not yet up, too early morning
Brings you like bells in matrix of mist
Noises the mind may finger, but no meaning.
Two blocks away a single car has crossed

Your intersection with the hour; each noise
A cough in the cathedral of your waking –
The cleaners have no souls, no sins – each does
Some job, Christ dying or the day breaking.

This you suppose is what goes on all day.
No one is allowed long to stop and listen,
But takes brief turns at it: now as you lie

Dead calm, one gust in the damp cedar hissing
Will have the mist right off in half a minute.
You will not grasp the meaning, you will be in it.

POLYNESIA

Surf is a partial deafness islanders
All suffer from, committed to the land;
A resonant hades, traversing, the fathers
Left cold or sweltering a world behind;

A drumming, drumming, drumming till there leapt
Fully afforested from the well of ocean
Valley and peak; the glove of blindness clapped
On trusting eyes; perpetual collision

Indistinguishable in those eyes,
Of salt of tears within and spray without;
Currents not warm or cold, of abstract seas
By any sense unfathomed, but where float

Small gods in shawls of bark, blind, numb, and deaf,
But buoyant, eastward in the blaze of surf.

THE NAVIGATORS

O rational successful hands that swept
Sea treasures up, by sunlight as in fog
Fumbling for islands, is there no wave big
Enough to wash your red ones green? O kept
In suavest history, gloved, quite dark how dipped
In red lagoons, the bright stain like a flag
Flowing and floating. Cradled in the vague
Currents where cables mumble murder slept

And sleeps, but dreams, hands that will not come clean
In endless dumb show utter what they did;
Because it was their rational violence
To think discreet discharge of guns would add
Island on island, that the seas would fence,
And time confirm them, in a change of scene.

SAILING OR DROWNING

In terms of some green myth, sailing or drowning,
Each day makes clear a statement to the next;
But to make out our tomorrow from its motives
Is pure guessing, yesterday's were so mixed.

Papa, Atea, parents of gods or islands,
Quickly forgave the treacherous beaches, none
So bloodily furrowed that the secret tides
Could not make the evening and the morning one.

Ambition has annulled that constitution;
In the solid sea and the space over the sea
Explosions of a complex origin
Shock, rock and split the memory.

Sailing or drowning, the living and the dead,
Less than the gist of what has just been said.

THE SKELETON OF THE GREAT MOA
IN THE CANTERBURY MUSEUM, CHRISTCHURCH

The skeleton of the moa on iron crutches
Broods over no great waste; a private swamp
Was where this tree grew feathers once, that hatches
Its dusty clutch, and guards them from the damp.

Interesting failure to adapt on islands,
Taller but not more fallen than I, who come
Bone to his bone, peculiarly New Zealand's.
The eyes of children flicker round this tomb

Under the skylights, wonder at the huge egg
Found in a thousand pieces, pieced together
But with less patience than the bones that dug
In time deep shelter against ocean weather:

Not I, some child, born in a marvellous year,
Will learn the trick of standing upright here.

THE OLD PROVINCIAL COUNCIL BUILDINGS,
CHRISTCHURCH

The steps are saucered in the trodden parts,
But that doesn't take long to happen here;
Two or three generations' traffic starts
In stone like this to make time's meaning clear.

Azaleas burn your gaze away below,
Corbel and finial tell you where to stop;
For present purposes, it does to know
Transport is licensed somewhere at the top.

Children of those who suffered a sea change
May wonder how much history was quarried
And carted, hoisted, carved; and find it strange
How shallow here their unworn age lies buried

Before its time, before their time, whose eyes
Get back from a stopped clock their own surprise.

AT JOACHIM KAHN'S

a quartet of Beethoven

Your 'innermost Beethoven' in the uttermost isles,
Half angel and half 'plane attains his peak
In weather like these southerlies that strike
But let your glass wall stand; his ceiling smiles;
He outclimbs all. Your room contains controls
To track in dazed skies an invisible wake
And pull his signals down just where you like,
It happens, among these unconnected hills.

The stone-deaf islands may resolve their pain
Easily, however distance howls them down,
By adaptation towards the albatross:
To rise on a stilled wing; or, on these tuned
Strings ride gales to patience; or, to cross
Motionless horizons as if not marooned.

RITE OF SPRING

Cold, limp with winter burial,
And mouldy with excessive rain,
My optimism shows no root
Now that I dig it up again.

Too easily the spade goes in,
Too heavily the spade heaves out;
A weekly tenant of the swamp,
I till in jest and plant in doubt.

I neither, between famous seas,
Dandle my idylls, island-graced,
Nor angrily enjoy a land
Not unequivocally waste.

Willow and lilac split the bud
And seagulls bray behind the plough:
This corm of courage shows no root,
The gilt is off that Golden Bough.

IN SUMMER SHEETED UNDER

In summer sheeted under
Acres of warm iron
We who drained our estate
Sleep in a wind, drying

The skin of our days,
Sucking our need of water
From private tanks, tapping
The secret strata.

Now is the confident season
For all exotic growth,
Fleshy of limb and leaf
Towards the blunted south.

Our clay is crusted, our
Tar sweats and shimmers;
Windows stand wide open
The desert of summer's

Pride, pride of our time
In a little dry dust;
Men but not as trees, walking
Fast, wordless. In a mist.

SPRING, 1942

A Letter to Sub-Lieutenant D.J.M. Glover, R.N.Z.N.V.R.

I walk to the Bryndwr bus
By the Wairarapa Stream,
Where a boy too young for an angler
Hooks trout too small to take;
With a Handel air in my head
(The radio just turned off)
And a book I shall not read
Because of the hills that hang
In the east, the shreds of thought and
Hopes that hang in my head.

I think, as I do now,
What do you think of islands
Who have made the formative journey
From antarctic to arctic –
Have laid yourself in the breech
Of this time's gun, to be fired
Into God knows what target?
In all that violent process
You follow the arc of islands.
The seas are shaping something.

In the bus rounding the river
Which the English think looks English
(Not reading between the willows)
I gaze through the jolting window,
Never expecting a symbol
To join our thought or reclaim
The undeniable oceans
That freeze or flame between us;
But you were the pine in the park,
The toughest, that we admired,
But could not establish the name.

And stopping between the colleges
Where over the mounded foliage
Of chestnuts, the six miles off
Hills shoulder the sun,
I wonder if half our worries
Were nineteenth-century Gothic.
These were the stones laid on us:
Did rebel imagination
Serve us no better than Samson's
Wrench, raving the roof down,
For building the City of God?

I did not expect a symbol,
Resigned to no sign given;
But the clock has stopped in the tower,
The ivy is stripped from the walls.
I have only to walk to work.
There is neither time nor money
For putting up sham pavilions;

Only the night's work
For me, battle or boredom
For you. O there will be poets
And there will be wars, and work,
And a child. You will return.

You wanted thoughts like the Arrow
River, and luminous
But never cold; you will have them.
'There is only hope for people
'Who live upon islands' – (no poet
Could mean just that, but something
Was in his mind at the time.)
All I can add in our case
Is, we do not choose our islands,
But mountains are magnets where
Our fathers sailed in under,
Heroes or hangdog exiles
Or (it doesn't matter) marooned.

The ivy is swept and burned
And the sallow clock has stopped
That would never keep good time.
One generation of exiles,
Two more of amphibious hauntings
Of beaches, and now this other
We needed to keep so badly.
O I could go down to harbours
And mourn with a hundred years
Of hunger what slips away there,
If that were not fearing the future.
Any day you may return.

PACIFIC THEATRE, 1943

World, up to now we've heard your hungers wail
No more than mock alerts; a South Seas moon
Unspeckled by our deaths can safely sail,
Escorted by our Never past our Soon.

The great sad duchess by a trick saw pass
Shapes of her husband and her children dead;
But farther off, darker than in a glass,
The natural body of our grief is read.

Men of our islands and our blood returning
Broken or whole, can still be reticent;
They do not wear that face we are discerning
As in a mirror momentarily lent,

A glitter that might be pride, an ashy glow
That could be pity, if the shapes would show.

IN MEMORIAM

2/Lieutenant T.C.F. Ronalds

Weeping for bones in Africa, I turn
Our youth over like a dead bird in my hand.
This unexpected personal concern
That what has character can simply end

Is my unsoldierlike acknowledgement
Cousin, to you, once gentle-tough, inert
Now, after the death-flurry of that front
Found finished too. And why should my report

Cry one more hero, winking through its tears?
I would say, you are cut off, and mourn for that;
Because history where it destroys admires,
But O if your blood's tongued it must recite

South Island feats, those tall snow-country tales
Among incredulous Tunisian hills.

TO M.H. HOLCROFT

That silence in the hills suggested neither
Prayer Book nor Year Book nor our games could save us,
For all the manly noise we made together;
Plainly the mountain would not move or move us.

The dead were burying their dead so deep
No roots could reach them; mostly we behaved
As if the country shamed us with a shape
Too trite or terrible to be believed.

Now all the history that did not happen
Begins, and stings like an unfrozen wound;
Beaches are barbed, the obvious roads lie open
Towards those foothills, Monte, where you found

Spiritual powers, but root and rock to grip;
For islands, an intelligible hope.

LANDFALL IN UNKNOWN SEAS

*The 300th Anniversary of the Discovery of New Zealand
by Abel Tasman, 13 December, 1642*

I

Simply by sailing in a new direction
You could enlarge the world.
                    You picked your captain,
Keen on discoveries, tough enough to make them,
Whatever vessels could be spared from other
More urgent service for a year's adventure;
Took stock of the more probable conjectures
About the Unknown to be traversed, all
Guesses at golden coasts and tales of monsters
To be digested into plain instructions
For likely and unlikely situations.

All this resolved and done, you launched the whole
On a fine morning, the best time of year,
Skies widening and the oceanic furies
Subdued by summer illumination; time
To go and to be gazed at going
On a fine morning, in the Name of God
Into the nameless waters of the world.

O you had estimated all the chances
Of business in those waters, the world's waters
Yet unexploited.
                        But more than the sea-empire's
Cannon, the dogs of bronze and iron barking
From Timor to the Straits, backed up the challenge.
Between you and the South an older enmity
Lodged in the searching mind, that would not tolerate
So huge a hegemony of ignorance.
There, where your Indies had already sprinkled
Their tribes like ocean rains, you aimed your voyage;
Like them invoked your God, gave seas to history
And islands to new hazardous tomorrows.

                        II

Suddenly exhilaration
Went off like a gun, the whole
Horizon, the long chase done,
Hove to. There was the seascape
Crammed with coast, surprising
As new lands will, the sailor
Moving on the face of the waters,
Watching the earth take shape
Round the unearthly summits, brighter
Than its emerging colour.

Yet this, no far fool's errand,
Was less than the heart desired,
In its old Indian dream
The glittering gulfs ascending
Past palaces and mountains
Making one architecture.

Here the uplifted structure,
Peak and pillar of cloud –
O splendour of desolation – reared
Tall from the pit of the swell,
With a shadow, a finger of wind, forbade
Hopes of a lucky landing.

Always to islanders danger
Is what comes over the sea;
Over the yellow sands and the clear
Shallows, the dull filament
Flickers, the blood of strangers:
Death discovered the Sailor
O in a flash, in a flat calm,
A clash of boats in the bay
And the day marred with murder.
The dead required no further
Warning to keep their distance;
The rest, noting the failure,
Pushed on with a reconnaissance
To the north; and sailed away.

III

Well, home is the Sailor, and that is a chapter
In a schoolbook, a relevant yesterday
We thought we knew all about, being much apter
        To profit, sure of our ground,
No murderers mooring in our Golden Bay.

But now there are no more islands to be found
And the eye scans risky horizons of its own
In unsettled weather, and murmurs of the drowned
        Haunt their familiar beaches –
Who navigates us towards what unknown

But not improbable provinces? Who reaches
A future down for us from the high shelf
Of spiritual daring? Not those speeches
        Pinning on the Past like a decoration
For merit that congratulates itself,

O not the self-important celebration
Or most painstaking history, can release
The current of a discoverer's elation
    And silence the voices saying,
'Here is the world's end where wonders cease'.

Only by a more faithful memory, laying
On him the half-light of a diffident glory,
The Sailor lives, and stands beside us, paying
    Out into our time's wave
The stain of blood that writes an island story.

from
Island and Time
(1941)

SENTENCE

Tentative the houses
Unhaunted over tombs;
Wind shakes the standing
Timber, shakes rooms
Where cold under *rimu*
Rafters they discover
The wind wet with change, and
The stranger for lover.

COUNTRY SCHOOL

You know the school; you call it old –
Scrub-worn floors and paint all peeled
On barge-board, weatherboard and gibbet belfry.

Pinus betrays, with rank tufts topping
The roof-ridge, scattering bravely
Nor'west gale as a reef its waves
While the small girls squeal at skipping
And magpies hoot from the eaves.

For scantling *Pinus* stands mature
In less than the life of a man;
The rusty saplings, the school, and you
Together your lives began.

O sweet antiquity! Look, the stone
That skinned your knees. How small
Are the terrible doors; how sad the dunny
And the things you drew on the wall.

HOUSE AND LAND

Wasn't this the site, asked the historian,
Of the original homestead?
Couldn't tell you, said the cowman;
I just live here, he said,
Working for old Miss Wilson
Since the old man's been dead.

Moping under the bluegums
The dog trailed his chain
From the privy as far as the fowlhouse
And back to the privy again,
Feeling the stagnant afternoon
Quicken with the smell of rain.

There sat old Miss Wilson,
With her pictures on the wall,
The baronet uncle, mother's side,
And the one she called The Hall;
Taking tea from a silver pot
For fear the house might fall.

People in the *colonies*, she said,
Can't quite understand . . .
Why, from Waiau to the mountains
It was all father's land.

She's all of eighty said the cowman,
Down at the milking-shed.
I'm leaving here next winter.
Too bloody quiet, he said.

The spirit of exile, wrote the historian,
Is strong in the people still.
He reminds me rather, said Miss Wilson,
Of Harriet's youngest, Will.

The cowman, home from the shed, went drinking
With the rabbiter home from the hill.

The sensitive nor'west afternoon
Collapsed, and the rain came;
The dog crept into his barrel
Looking lost and lame.
But you can't attribute to either
Awareness of what great gloom
Stands in a land of settlers
With never a soul at home.

THE UNHISTORIC STORY

Whaling for continents coveted deep in the south
The Dutchman envied the unknown, drew bold
Images of market-place, populous rivermouth,
The Land of Beach ignorant of the value of gold:
    Morning in Murderers' Bay
    Blood drifted away.
    It was something different, something
    Nobody counted on.

Spider, clever and fragile, Cook showed how
To spring a trap for islands, turning from planets
His measuring mission, showed what the musket could do,
Made his Christmas goose of the wild gannets.
    Still as the collier steered
    No continent appeared;
    It was something different, something
    Nobody counted on.

The roving tentacles touched, rested, clutched
Substantial earth, that is, accustomed haven
For the hungry whaler. Some inland, some hutched
Rudely in bays, the shaggy foreshore shaven,
    Lusted, preached as they knew;
    But as the children grew
    It was something different, something
    Nobody counted on.

Green slashed with flags, pipeclay and boots in the bush,
Christ in a canoe and the musketed Maori boast;
All a rubble-rattle at Time's glacial push:
Vogel and Seddon howling empire from an empty coast
   A vast ocean laughter
   Echoed unheard, and after
   All it was different, something
   Nobody counted on.

The pilgrim dream pricked by a cold dawn died
Among the chemical farmers, the fresh towns; among
Miners, not husbandmen, who piercing the side
Let the land's life, found like all who had so long
   Bloodily or tenderly striven
   To rearrange the given,
   It was something different, something
   Nobody counted on.

After all re-ordering of old elements
Time trips up all but the humblest of heart
Stumbling after the fire, not in the smoke of events;
For many are called, but many are left at the start,
   And whatever islands may be
   Under or over the sea,
   It is something different, something
   Nobody counted on.

A VICTIM

*Jan Tyssen, one of the four Dutch killed by Maori when
   Tasman anchored in Murderers' Bay in 1642*

No prey for prowling keels, the south
We found a monster risky to rouse
That at the first approach bared teeth
And slew four with terrible blows.

I, Jan Tyssen, company's sailor,
Shipped aboard Zeehaen from Batavia,
Gerrit Janz master; signed to follow
Bully Tasman, lands to discover.

Java to Mauritius were orders, then
Southward far to the fabulous coast:
Glory to captains, to our masters gain;
To us reward as pleased them best.

Grim under earth the gale-black sea
Spat us between ice-tainted lips;
Heemskirck, Zeehaen, denied that way,
With fair winds eastward bore our hopes:

Mountains stood up (I, Tyssen, now
Remember all thickly through the black
Swoon of the savage's thrust) below
Clouted, thin lipped, a dull surf spoke.

This land we coasted, came on a bay
Calm where canoes slid slim at sunset;
Wary we waited, heard a hollow voice cry,
None came near, nor omen of onset:

Morning brought more canoes; we made
Offer of mirrors, good iron pots,
As orders were; only the tide
Plucked by paddles, and hoarse shouts

Answered. I, one of seven, was told
'Take Zeehaen's boat, pull to your ship'.
(Ah, with what bells is my brain filled
That I forget!) We crossed the gap

Green between hulls. Like devils drove
Cruel of our kind the dark-limbed crew;
Blood bloomed and vanished where the wave
Mouthed for the fruit of us they slew.

I, Tyssen, first blood to the south,
Turned Tasman from that hateful haven.
Your history's cold, and cold's my death,
Past pity, past anger, past forgiving.

TIME

I am the nor'west air nosing among the pines
I am the water-race and the rust on railway lines
I am the mileage recorded on the yellow signs.

I am dust, I am distance, I am lupins back of the beach
I am the sums the sole-charge teachers teach
I am cows called to milking and the magpie's screech.

I am nine o'clock in the morning when the office is clean
I am the slap of the belting and the smell of the machine
I am the place in the park where the lovers were seen.

I am recurrent music the children hear
I am level noises in the remembering ear
I am the sawmill and the passionate second gear.

I, Time, am all these, yet these exist
Among my mountainous fabrics like a mist,
So do they the measurable world resist.

I, Time, call down, condense, confer
On the willing memory the shapes these were:
I, more than your conscious carrier,

Am island, am sea, am father, farm, and friend,
Though I am here all things my coming attend;
I am, you have heard it, the Beginning and the End.

ST THOMAS'S RUINS

Bishop George Selwyn grew tired of wood;
Like Solomon he desired permanent materials,
Home comforts for his traveller God,
Cypress and spire, background for burials.

So rock hardly cool from the crater
Assumed devout posture; column and arch
Housed the Lord fittingly and to the better
Credit of His bride the Church.

But ocean weather sucked the ill-mixed mortar
In as many years as the Norman's nave
Had centuries falling; sand, faith's deserter,
Made paste for rain to grind his groove.

Ubi episcopus, ibi ecclesia. The storm
Outgunned in grace the Bishop's praying,
Blew to his knees the seed of this cabbage-palm
Whose tufted rood transfixes the toy ruin.

WILD IRON

Sea go dark, dark with wind,
Feet go heavy, heavy with sand,
Thoughts go wild, wild with the sound
Of iron on the old shed swinging, clanging:
Go dark, go heavy, go wild, go round,
    Dark with the wind,
    Heavy with the sand,
Wild with the iron that tears at the nail
And the foundering shriek of the gale.

Notes

A BUSY PORT (p.9)

The time-ball tower housed 'a sphere which at a certain moment each day is allowed to fall down a vertical rod placed in a prominent position, so as to give an accurate indication of time' (*New Shorter Oxford Dictionary*). At the port of Lyttelton, New Zealand, my busy port, it is a gothic-looking affair, the crenellated main turret supporting the ball and rod. There were quarters for (I imagine) the signalman who, as well as attending to the ball, hoisted flags on the adjacent flagpole, to announce and identify ships arriving off the Heads. The ball itself was for ships in port to correct their chronometers by. Technology will have changed all this, but the tower remains.

ANOTHER WEEKEND AT THE BEACH (p.10)

kina, line 28: the edible sea-urchin *Evechinus chloroticus*. Maori loanword.

LOOKING WEST, LATE AFTERNOON, LOW WATER (p.14)

Tangaroa, line 24: Maori god of the sea, supreme god in some other parts of Oceania, or creator of the world.

THE SCRAP-BOOK (p.16)

Eighty-three pages are left, of the hundred or so the scrap-book had when William Woon wrote his entries in it, being storm-bound at my great-great-grandfather Peter Monro's house on the Hokianga in October 1841. It has lost one of its heavy black embossed covers, and its spine. Many pages are blank, others haphazardly occupied by sentimental verses, sketches, engravings of ships, houses, horses, clipped or copied from books or albums of the time. Woon's entries take one full page; another is filled by a pencil sketch of 'Horeke, from Manungu, Hokianga', where the stockades of Maori *paa* (strongholds) appear on hilltops across the water, and a *waka* (war canoe) paddles up the harbour past a small house in European style with its fence-posts behind the beach. Woon, a Wesleyan missionary, returned on 11 September 1844, to open the book again where he had written three years ago: he asterisked the earlier date, and added a pious couplet, still in the darker oscillation of his evangelical faith: '*See the rapid flight of time – How it swiftly runs away! / May we now His favour seek – While it yet is called day!*'

I, line 17: Ngapuhi country. Dominant Maori tribe of northernmost New Zealand.

II, lines 9-10: *iwi* of the *tangata whenua*: literally 'tribes of the people of the land'. Common borrowings in New Zealand English.

EARLY DAYS YET (p.18)
The petrol tank of these cars was mounted under the high front seat, so that fuel reached the engine by simple gravity feed. A cost advantage, no doubt, over other cars of the period, though not without inconvenience to driver and passenger, who had to get out whenever filling was necessary. The gravity system could fail when climbing an exceptionally steep slope: the resourceful driver would then turn the car round, and proceed in reverse.

A FACING PAGE (p.21)
In Stoker's story it was a city stricken by plague. Another illustration showed a very old man and a very young girl seated on the edge of a fountain in a public square. One of them, I forget which, holds out a consoling hand to the other.

PACIFIC 1945-1995 (p.24)
The three words in quotation marks, quatrains 10-11 of this poem, are a theft from Robert Penn Warren's great Hiroshima poem, 'New Dawn'. My pantoum appeared also in *Below the Surface, Words and Images in Protest at French Testing on Moruroa* (Random House New Zealand Ltd, Auckland, 1995).

AN EVENING LIGHT (p.26)
The Ngai-tahu tribe (lines 25-6) occupied, and still claim, a great part of the South Island of New Zealand. A *Kainga* is a Maori settlement, a *paa* was a fortified (stockaded) place or stronghold. In common European speech, *paa* is often used for any form of Maori settlement; infrequently and locally, *kainga* is heard in the corrupt form 'kaik'.

ON THE ROAD TO EREWHON (p.45)
A few lines and parts of lines are lifted, unaltered, from Butler's *Erewhon*, Chapter 5, 'The River and the Range'. The young Butler's four New Zealand years (1859-1863) were spent sheep-farming on his own high-country station between the headwaters of the Rakaia and Rangitata rivers, flowing east from the Southern Alps to the Pacific Ocean; he called his land Mesopotamia, after the 'between rivers' of antiquity, and the name has stuck, at least for the trifle of another century and a quarter. Anyone born and bred, as I was, in sight of the same sea and mountains, enjoys privileged access to the region of Butler's opening chapters, drawn (as he tells us) from 'the Upper Rangitata district of the Canterbury Province (as it then was) of New Zealand'. It is a common terrain and climate: its mountains, rivers, and winds are the outdoors bearings of other poems I have

collected here, 'A Sight for Sore Eyes', 'A Raised Voice', 'An Evening Light', 'A Time of Day'. The terrifying statues guard the summit of the pass which Butler's narrator crosses, from the landscapes of reality, westward into the 'nowhere' of *Erewhon*. On which plane does he (or Butler) hear, back in England and telling his story, the bars of a Handel prelude, printed in the text, which remind him of the 'horrible' aeolian blasts of the Erewhonian statues?

BLIND MAN'S HOLIDAY (p.47)

I. The packets of Utamaro postcards any traveller can buy at a Japanese airport contain no examples of the eighteenth-century master's erotic art; nor do historians (I suppose) connect this genre peculiarly with the name of his Western contemporary Henry Fuseli, the adoptive name, that is, of the Swiss-born Johann Heinrich Füssli. It is a somewhat circumscribed modern taste which discovers them both in, say, some production of the Erotic Art Book Society – in company with Rembrandt, Rowlandson, Grosz, Balthus, Dali, and Picasso. Does anybody know whether Sacheverell Sitwell guessed correctly that 'hundreds of these exceptionable drawings may have escaped Mrs Fuseli's kitchen-range'? Or how deeply scandalized friends like Flaxman and Haydon actually were, learning of their existence at the time of the artist's death in 1825? My source is Eudo C. Mason, *The Mind of Henry Fuseli* (London, 1951), citing Benjamin Haydon's *Diary* and Allan Cunningham's *Life* of Fuseli.

II. A First World War early childhood left a few of Bairnsfather's popular cartoons of trench warfare sharply printed on my memory. *The Queen's Gift Book* would be one of those sumptuously got up volumes published under royal patronage in aid of patriotic funds; there were cosmetic paintings of scenes at the Front, like the retreat from Mons, in the lurid colour reproduction of the time.

III. Alvin Lucier's 'long wire' was on loan to the Auckland City Art Gallery for a time in 1984, a wonderful contrivance, not only for the electronically translated sounds intended by the American composer, but visually as well. Voices or footsteps in the gallery, noises in the street outside, made a continuously changing murmur about almost everything. Not mere 'electro-acoustic natural photography' as someone described Luc Ferrari's *Daybreak on the Beach*: much nearer, even painfully, to one's sole self.

A FELLOW BEING (p.65)

For 'A Fellow Being' I helped myself to detail from Dick Scott's account of F.J. Rayner (*Fire on the Clay*, Auckland, 1979) which also refreshed a memory of remarks by Aucklanders of an older generation. Of course, the historian is not answerable for the poet's conceptions. My uses of Eliot R. Davis's memoir (*A Link with the Past*, 1948) are, I think, self-explanatory.

A PASSION FOR TRAVEL (p.80)
pakeha: Maori loan-word, for 'not Maori' viz. 'European', or 'introduced', 'not indigenous'.

ORGANO AD LIBITUM (p.89)
I. The quoted lines are grafts from *Erewhon*, Chapter 4 (see note to 'On the Road to Erewhon' above). The parish organ changes to the mountainous instrument played by the transfigured Handel of Butler's dream, but this is 'no dreme, I lay brode waking': the cadaver is 'wide awake' to the knowledge of death, as it recites the erotic mystery of Wyatt's sixteenth-century sonnet. *Taihoa*! Maori loan-word for 'wait a bit' or 'no hurry'.
II. The film is Walerian Borowczyk's *Intérieur d'un Couvent*, the quoted poem Gerard Manley Hopkins': 'To What Serves Mortal Beauty'.
IV. The 'boulder of Magritte', a detail of 'Le Cap des Tempêtes', adorns the cover of my paperback copy of Camus's *The Myth of Sisyphus*.
V. The antarctic volcano is Mt Erebus, on which an Air New Zealand DC10 crashed on a sightseeing flight, killing nearly 300 passengers and crew.
VIII. For 'Panurge said' see Rabelais, *Gargantua and Pantagruel*, Book III, chapter xviii (tr. Urquhart, 1693): 'Panurge is a second Bacchus, he hath been twice born . . . In him is renewed and begun again the palintokis of the Megarians, and the palingenesis of Democritus . . .' For Schopenhauer, see *Parerga and Paralipomena* (tr. Hollingdale): '. . . a clear distinction between *metempsychosis* . . . and *palingenesis*, which is the *decomposition* and reconstruction of the individual in which *will* alone persists and, assuming the shape of a new being, receives a new intellect'.
IX. Domenico Parrani smoked the biggest Savinelli pipe in Italy, and had some official role in the denomination of the country's wines. One day we (my wife and I) drove with him along the north Sicilian coast from Capo Skino to Capo d'Orlando, where it amazed him that we took our *espressi* without the usual sugar.

A BALANCED BAIT IN HANDY PELLET FORM (p.103)
The Torlesse range (line 11) rises to *c.* 6,000 feet, east of the main divide of the Southern Alps, to dominate this part of the Canterbury

(New Zealand) plains. Cf. my poems 'A Time of Day' and 'Early Days Yet', also 'On the Road to Erewhon' and my Note to that poem. The 'other poet' (line 31) is Byron, *Childe Harold's Pilgrimage*, canto IV, cxxvi.

THINGS TO DO WITH MOONLIGHT (p.116)

'Karekare doppelgänger' (line 58) names the place (Karekare) where the poem was written, on the steeply forested coast of the Tasman Sea, west of Auckland; I have spent most of my summers and weekends there since 1961. All four syllables are sounded, rather like English 'carry-carry'; a native (or instructed) Maori speaker might give the vowels different values, more like Italian, and stress the word differently. This Note is for the sake of the metre, since the name occurs elsewhere in these poems (v. 'Moro Assassinato', I, and 'A Fellow Being'. II, VI, VII, IX).

MORO ASSASSINATO (p.119)

Parts of this poem inevitably owe a good deal to the Italian press, but in particular to the Naples daily *Il Mattino*, of 9 May 1978; to the news magazine *Panorama*, Milan, 13 June 1978; to *Corriere della Sera*, of 13 September 1978 (for seven letters of Moro, posthumously published). The German magazine *Stern* interviewed Michael Baumann (see motto of 'II. *An Urban Guerrilla*) in an 'underground hideout'; my source is an English translation of this interview, in *Encounter*, September 1978.

The character of the sequence *An Incorrigible Music* was decided, and most of the poems written, some months earlier than the kidnapping of Aldo Moro in the Via Fani, Rome, with the death of his five guards, on 16 March 1978. It was impossible to live in Italy from early April through June, reading the newspapers, catching the mood from chance remarks or no remarks at all, and not be affected. To this day, nobody knows where the 'Prison of the People' was. At the spot in Via Caetani Rome, where the murdered man's body was left, in the Renault 4, about a dozen metres of wall were covered with private tokens of respect – handwritten papers, placards, flowers _ from the ground to above head height. People came and went, or stood silently. That was mid-June, a full month later.

AN ABOMINABLE TEMPER (p. 143)

My great-great-grandfather Peter Monro (1793-1865) settled in the far north of New Zealand in 1835, five years earlier than the Treaty of Waitangi, by which Maori chiefs ceded a putative sovereignty to

Queen Victoria, beginning the colonial period of New Zealand's history. His son's letter, written in old age to one of my father's aunts, is my primary source (see the headnote to the poem). His *Poetical Works* of Burns is on my bookshelf, in remarkably good repair, considering its many sea voyages and at least one fire since he bought and inscribed it, *c.* 1812, in Edinburgh. See also my Note to 'The Scrap-book', above.

TREES, EFFIGIES, MOVING OBJECTS (p.153)

If I say these poems were written in the spring and summer of 1971 and 1972, I mean that is when they were finished and found the order in which they now appear. A poet never stops trying to save poetry from poetry, to make something of it, not a spurious everything. Memory is always something, but if memory were ever good enough – even a moment ago! – would we want poetry? Isn't this the necessary irritant? Because of it, memory is a thing of the present, a thing of the future too, if that is not already taken care of. It was in fact ten years earlier, the spring and summer of 1961, which I spent in Washington D.C., that the first notes for parts of this sequence were made: in particular II 'Friendship Heights', X 'A Framed Photograph', 'XIV 'Bourdon'. In XIII 'A Four Letter Word' the Maori names (line 3) are of trees in the New Zealand rainforest. *Tane* is the tree-god in Maori theogony: he raised the sky-father (Rangi) from the earth-mother (Papa) so that his fellow divinities had living space between. He is *Tane mahuta* (Tane arisen, or rising) in the form of the bole of a great *kauri* in the Waipoua forest, much visited by tourists though decayed over centuries.

IN MEMORY OF DYLAN THOMAS (p. 195)

When Dylan Thomas died in 1953, Charles Brasch asked me to write a memoir for *Landfall*. It was three years since Ruth Witt and I had seen Thomas off at the San Francisco airport: he returning east, and I, a few days later, to sail for New Zealand. It was not the time, and perhaps not the place either, for me to attempt any connected account of what I had known of him, our meetings in London in 1949, a week with him in Wales the same year, our experiences together (memorable enough, though not much in the way of stories that have lost too little in the telling) in America during 1950. The poem sprang from the feeling that I was not let off. It appeared in *Landfall*, with some photographs – snaps of us both by Caitlin with my cheap box camera – for sufficient explanation that it was written in part from personal recollection. When it was reprinted in *A Garland for Dylan*

Thomas (New York, 1963) I added a brief note in place of the photographs. Neither should be needed today; but I remember a friend's warning, that some readers might mistake me: there was a flood of poetic tributes in those years.

LANDFALL IN UNKNOWN SEAS (p. 226)

Early in 1942, I was asked to write a poem to commemorate the 300th anniversary of Tasman's first sighting of New Zealand, falling on 13 December of that year. It was a commission from the National Historical Branch of New Zealand Internal Affairs, under the guidance of J.C. Beaglehole, OM, historian of Pacific exploration and editor of Cook's *Journals*. There was to be a commemorative book, consisting of a new essay by Beaglehole, a new translation of the Dutch navigator's log, and my poem, all under the title *Abel Janszoon Tasman and the Discovery of New Zealand*. Once this was on its way into print, I showed the poem to the composer Douglas Lilburn, hoping it would strike him as a subject for music, and by great good fortune it did. The first performance of the narrated poem, wonderfully complemented and illuminated by Lilburn's music for string orchestra, took place in Wellington on 13 December 1942. I have not counted all the performances since – in New Zealand alone, one or more every year for the fifty-odd years – broadcasts and recordings, the latest on CD.

THE UNHISTORIC STORY (p. 235)

'The Land of Beach . . .' This reference, with others in the same poem, I have from J.C. Beaglehole's *Exploration of the Pacific*. From seventeenth-century Dutch sources the author gives examples of the belief in a fabulously rich country or continent somewhere in the south. Frederick de Houtman, coming on the west coast of Australia, thought 'that this must be the coastline of the "Beach" or "Locach" of Marco Polo, with its fabulous riches'. Visscher, Tasman's chief adviser, planned the discovery of 'all the utterly unknown provinces of Beach'. Gold was thought to be abundant there, and some hoped to profit by the inhabitants' supposed ignorance of its value.

'Vogel and Seddon howling empire . . .' Sir Julius Vogel and Richard John Seddon, late nineteenth-century premiers of New Zealand. They sought 'wholesale annexations' of Pacific island territories by Britain: there were dreams of an oceanic empire under New Zealand rule.

A VICTIM (p. 236)
The occasion of this poem, if not the impulse, and some narrative detail, I owe to J.C. Beaglehole, *The Discovery of New Zealand* (Wellington 1940) and to the portion of Tasman's journal quoted by him.

ST THOMAS'S RUINS (p.239)
By the St Helier's Bay road, Auckland, there stood in an open paddock the ruined and roofless walls of a small imitation-Gothic church, known as St Thomas's Ruins. The church was said to have been built by Bishop Selwyn, nostalgic for a place of worship recalling the stone churches of England. But it was ill-constructed; the mortar did not hold, so people said, because it was mixed with sea-sand. Ironically, Selwyn's timber churches, like the St John's College chapel near by, have lasted 150 years and longer.